THE
GOURMET
GUIDE
TO
BEER

THE
GOURMET
GUIDE
TO
BEER

Howard Hillman

Research/Editorial/Administrative Staff
Trudi Daub
Claire Curtin
Gloria Zimmerman

Facts On File Publications
New York, New York • Oxford, England

dedicated to lovers of quality beer

The Gourmet Guide to Beer

Copyright © 1987 by Howard Hillman

Library of Congress Cataloging-in-Publication Data
Hillman, Howard.
   The gourmet guide to beer.

   Bibliography: p.
   Includes index.
   1. Beer. I. Title.
TP577.H56 1987   641.2'3   86-32796
ISBN 0-8160-1600-3 (hc)
ISBN 0-8160-1862-6 (pb)

Composition by Facts On File/Maxwell Photographics.

Printed in the United States of America
10 9 8 7 6 5 4 3 2 1

CONTENTS

INTRODUCTION

Now is the time to become a discriminating activist in the American beer-drinking revolution. While the growth in sales of ordinary American beer is flatter than yesterday's leftover brew, the appreciation and consumption of quality beers is bubbling. Beer connoisseurship today is where that for wine was twenty years ago. Remember then? Most of us thought of wine as either red or white or, perhaps, dry or sweet. We've come a long way in wine appreciation.

Beer—that is, quality beer—is just as complex, varied and exciting as wine. Since I also write about wine, I believe I can make this comparison objectively. Beer connoisseurship is a worthy pursuit. Northern and Central Europeans have known this for centuries. A growing number of Americans are also finding this to be true, as evidenced by the number of small "boutique" breweries mushrooming across the land.

This book offers insider tips on judging, buying, storing and serving beer. From it you will also gain an understanding of such basics as how beer is made and classified, information essential to any true brew maven.

I did not write this book for beer snobs, nor for the undiscriminating six-pack guzzlers who collectively quaff most of the beer sold and, therefore, determine quality standards for the mass market. Rather, I wrote it for you, the individual who shares my unwavering conviction that quality beer deserves our consuming passion in the full figurative sense.

You might say that my research began before my first birthday when my grandmother playfully gave me my inaugural sip of beer. ("You loved it." she later confided.) As most teenagers, I drank my fair share of beer at high school parties, but my research didn't begin in earnest until I temporarily moved to Europe a quarter century ago. It was then that I discovered the fascinating pastime of exploring the pubs, Gasthäuser and other brew temples in England, Germany and other beer-brewing nations. I continued my quest and eventually tasted thousands of different brews in more than one hundred countries around the world, from Afghanistan to Zimbabwe, from metropolitan Munich to small villages in the Orient.

More recently, I retested all the beers rated in this book. I also conducted laboratory experiments to separate fact from myth, read the voluminous literature on beer, and interviewed countless brewers, importers, bartenders and other tradespersons here and abroad.

Perhaps someday we will meet over a brew in your favorite pub or tavern. I hope so.

Cheers!

HOWARD HILLMAN

PART ONE

BUYING, STORING AND SERVING TIPS

BUYING

Avoid Stores That Don't Refrigerate Their Beer

Of all the popular alcoholic beverages, beer is by far the most perishable. Unlike wine, but like milk, an unopened bottle or can of beer must be refrigerated to maintain its freshness. (Tell that to your local beer retailer who stocks his supply on open shelves and he will probably get either hopping mad or give you a look calling your sanity into question).

Unfortunately, most stores keep their beer on open shelves at room temperature. This error not only creates flaws, it also magnifies whatever defects a brew may have developed because of mistreatment on its long trek from the vat to the retailer. Too often, beer is transported in unrefrigerated cargo ships or trucks, unloaded and left for hours under the baking sun, or allowed to linger in hot warehouses and storage rooms.

Avoid Stores That Exhibit Their Beer Under Fluorescent Lighting

Most retailers store their beer where it is exposed to fluorescent light. This is lamentable. Fluorescent, but not incandescent, light chemically alters bottled beer, giving it an offensive, skunky odor. (Note: For the definitions of "skunky" and nearly 200 other words relevant to beer tasting, see the "Tasting Terms" chapter beginning on page 53.)

Avoid Stores That Display Their Beer in a Window

Sunlight does even more damage to beer than fluorescent lighting. I make it a rule never to buy brew from any retailer who places unopened beer bottles by a window. You can bet your paycheck that these bottles will probably be rotated back into the stock before the labels fade but not before the beer has acquired a disagreeable odor and flavor.

Avoid Stores That Have Slow-Moving Stocks

Buy your beer from a store with a fast merchandise turnover. This is especially critical when buying a slow-selling beer such as an obscure imported brand.

Some brewers claim their beers will stay perfectly fresh for up to six months. One claims eighteen months. Baloney! The shorter the period between brewery and glass, the fresher and better the beer will taste.

It is possible for a brewery to extend shelf life a few months by using pasteurization, microfiltering and chemical additives—but, unfortunately, at the expense of quality. The longevity of a beer also tends to increase in direct correlation with its alcoholic strength, darkness, sweetness and hop content (though hops do make beer vulnerable to skunkiness).

Look for the Freshest Beer on the Shelf

Some retailers systematically rotate their stock by placing the new bottles of a brand behind the unsold ones. Most outlets are not that conscientious and, thus, bottles and cans can sit on the shelf for months on end. Tip: avoid dusty containers.

I know a few consumers who have managed to decipher the dating codes of some of their favorite brands. These codes are usually presented as a series of letters and numbers (23X17B, for instance) imprinted on the label or case, or silkscreened or stamped on the bottom of a nonreturnable container. Sometimes the code appears as a pattern of notches cut along the edge of the label. If you can't crack the code James Bond style, ask the brewery or retailer (some outfits will divulge the information).

Another technique for selecting the freshest container is to be alert to subtle modification in the design, wording or color of the label of your favorite brand. Your friends who collect beer cans and labels will verify how frequently these barely noticeable revisions occur. For instance, the hue of the border on the label may be switched from blue to bluish green.

Choose Bottles over Cans

Cans impart a metallic flavor to beer, glass doesn't.

Suggested Experiment

Buy the identical brand in a bottle and in a can. Cross-taste them.

Metal can manufacturers like to promote the fact that cans are quick cooling. They don't tell you the other and more important fact: cans are quick warming. That means canned beer may become too warm by the time you pour a final measure while watching the baseball game on TV.

Suggested Experiment

Cool both a bottled and a canned beer in the refrigerator. Then place them unopened on a table for 20 minutes. Pour the beers and note the difference in their temperatures.

Cans do have two pluses: they are lighter than bottles and they won't shatter. But these benefits hardly compensate for the metallic flavor cans impart and the rapid warming they encourage, nor do cans allow you to examine the color and clarity of the beer before opening them. Fortunately, beer cans are an endangered species and may become relatively extinct within the next five to ten years. It costs a brewer several cents more to package beer in a can than it does in a bottle—and this price differential is expected to increase.

If the brand you want is available only in a can, it is especially important that the brew be as factory-fresh as possible. The longer the beer sits in the can, the more metallic it will taste.

Shun Plastic Bottles

A beer stored in a plastic bottle becomes flatter more quickly than one stored in a glass container. Because plastic is permeable, carbonation escapes more readily.

Tinted Bottles Are Superior to Clear Ones

Beer bottles are tinted brown or green for a reason. Coloration helps (but does not totally) screen out damaging fluorescent lighting and sunlight. Brown is the slightly more opaque of the two colors.

In spite of the proven screening properties of tinted glass, some brewers, like Miller and Samuel Smith, use clear bottles for aesthetic reasons. Beer looks more attractive when packaged in a transparent container. This packaging is regrettable because clear glass increases the chance of a beer becoming skunky.

Twist-Off Caps Are Convenient, but . . .

A twist-off cap saves the day when you are without a bottle opener. However, compared to the traditional cap, it is more prone to leakage and, therefore, there is a greater likelihood that the beer will have gone flat or become oxidized before you even put it in your shopping cart.

Pick Up and Examine the Bottle

Ullage is the airspace between the liquid and the bottle's cap. If it is more than approximately one and one-half inches in a standard-sized bottle, don't buy that particular container. Not only will you be getting less beer than you are paying for, the extra volume of air will accelerate oxidation, giving the beer an off odor and flavor.

Should you suspect that a bottle of pale-hued beer has been around a long time, lift it up to a bright light and gently turn it upside down. If it is cloudy or has sediment, the beer is over-the-hill, unless you are holding a wheat or bottle-conditioned brew. (I discuss this concept in Part Two, "How to Judge the Beer in Your Hand.")

Don't Economize When Buying Beer

The price difference between a lowly Château Swampwater wine and a celebrated Château Lafite-Rothschild wine can be a hundred dollars. The cost gap between the world's worst and best beers is usually about fifty cents in a retail store and one dollar in a bar. This premium is meager considering the extra pleasure you gain. If you need to economize, I suggest you do it elsewhere.

There is, however, a point of diminishing return. Some greedy bars take outrageous markups on both their imported and domestic beers. On occasion I have been asked to pay more than five dollars for a beer that cost the owner less than one dollar. The Chutzpah Award, though, goes to a Californian who solicited bids for a bottle of 1968 vintage Thomas Hardy English Ale. His advertisement proclaimed that the minimum bid was one thousand dollars.

STORING

Don't Agitate the Beer

Baby your beer at all times, whether carrying it home from the store, transferring it to your refrigerator or bringing it to the table. Excessive agitation not only increases the carbon dioxide pressure in the bottle, it can foster chemical reactions that will alter the aroma and flavor of the beer.

Don't store the beer on the door shelf of your refrigerator. The frequent opening and closing of this door can be a jolting experience.

Even the gentlest of handling will agitate beer to some extent. To minimize the chance of accidentally spraying your tablemates with beer, don't open the bottle the day you lug it home from the store. A day's rest gives the newly built-up gas pressure in the airspace an opportunity to work itself back into the liquid.

Store the Bottle in the Refrigerator or in a Cool, Dark Place

Excessive heat hastens a beer's downfall. Damage will occur at even 70°F, but at 100°F (cooler than the trunk of your car on a sunny summer day) the injury is devastating. Just as you wouldn't want to buy beer off open shelves, you wouldn't want to store it in a warm place once you get it home.

Temperature fluctuations are also detrimental. These would occur if a beer were transferred in and out of the refrigerator several times.

The ideal storage temperature for nearly all the beers you will encounter is in the 40°F to 50°F zone. Your best bet is the warmest shelf in your refrigerator.

The brewers of certain beers, like the Belgian Trappist ales, recommend that you don't refrigerate their products at all. But unless you have a cool 55°F cellar (closets are usually too warm), these brews are best kept in the refrigerator.

Store Beer Bottles Upright, Not on Their Sides

Unlike a cork-topped bottle of wine, a metal-capped bottle of beer should be stored vertically rather than horizontally. Otherwise, the beer would come in contact with the metal lid and pick up a metallic flavor. A second, but overrated, reason for standing beer bottles upright is to hinder oxidation by minimizing the surface area between the enclosed air and the beer in the bottle.

Don't Store Beer for Extended Periods

I drink my beers within one week after bringing them home. Except for rare brews like the lambics of Belgium which sometimes need to be aged like wine, a bottle of beer is ready to drink by the time it reaches your local retail store. Even if you stashed it away in the most ideal of storage environments, the beer would slowly but perceptibly begin to develop flaws.

Don't Quick-Chill Beer in the Freezer

A sudden drop in temperature destroys some of the desirable sensory qualities in beer. Make it a point to allow sufficient time for a beer to chill relatively slowly in the warmest part of your refrigerator. This will usually take 45 minutes to an hour and a quarter, depending on the beer's original temperature, the desired serving temperature, the dial setting and location of the beer in your refrigerator and the size and material of the container. Also, sweet and full-bodied brews take longer to chill than their opposite numbers.

There's another reason why the freezer quick-chilling method should be avoided. If you forget to remove the beer (which you will sooner or later do), the container may explode, creating both a mess and a hazard. Light-bodied or low-alcohol beers are particularly troublesome because they freeze at higher temperatures than do their counterparts.

In a pinch you can compromise with a safe, quick-chilling method: submerge the beer in a bucket or tub of ice water for 20 to 40 minutes. This technique zaps far less quality than the freezer method.

SERVING

Serve Beer at Its Proper Temperature

Most Americans drink their beer too cold, usually in the 35°F to 40°F range. Pity.

There are two major disadvantages to serving beer too cold. You will not be able to enjoy all the subtleties of a brew because the low temperature numbs your taste buds and inhibits the release of aromatics from the beer. Secondly, the carbon dioxide will likely end up as a belch rather than as a soaring head because it will not be able to escape from its liquid prison as readily as it could at a higher temperature.

The ideal serving temperature varies according to the style of beer. Here are rough guidelines:

CATEGORY	TEMPERATURE
Ordinary Beers	40°F to 45°F
Quality Lagers	45°F to 50°F
Quality Ales	50°F to 55°F
Quality Stouts and Porters	55°F to 60°F

The wisdom behind these recommendations will become readily apparent if you cross-taste three bottles of the same brand. Serve the first at its proper serving temperature, the second 10°F colder and the third 10°F warmer. Note the differences in head sizes as well as in the strength and character of the aromas and flavors.

Ordinary beers can be served in the somewhat palate-numbing temperature range of 40°F to 45°F because they have few subtleties worth savoring. A temperature much greater than

45°F only magnifies their sensory flaws, and one below 40°F guarantees you a gassy belly.

Quality lagers that are well hopped (Beck's, for instance) are best appreciated at the lower limit of the 45°F to 50°F zone. Mildly hopped ones (the Munich versions) are best enjoyed at the upper limit of the quality lager serving temperature range.

Quality ales that are pale are at their finest at 50°F. The figure is 55°F for dark ales. An intermediate temperature suits amber ales. Trash the widely publicized belief that Britishers drink their beer warm. My exploratory pub trips through the various regions of Merry Olde England have confirmed that the British drink beer "warm" only by American standards. Few of the sampled brews measured higher than 60°F on my portable Taylor thermometer.

Porters in general and sweet stouts, like Mackeson, in particular come off best at 55°F. For dry stouts, the ideal temperature is 60°F. (Though 55°F is preferred for the bottled Guinness because it is more bitter than the unpasteurized draft variety found in Ireland.)

Wheat beers (*weiss* and *weizen*) are customarily served in Germany in the 50°F to 60°F zone. On particularly scorching days, however, 45°F is not uncommon.

If you have stored a quality brew in the refrigerator for any appreciable length of time, it will likely be too cold, and you will need to remove it from the unit ahead of serving time. When taking standard-size bottles from the warmest shelf of my refrigerator (45°F), I allow approximately 15 minutes for quality lagers, 25 minutes for quality ales and 40 minutes for quality stouts and porters. The periods need to be adjusted in keeping with the current temperature of the room and with the particular beer selected—for instance, a pale or a dark ale. I must also insert into the equation this factor: sweet and full-bodied beers warm at a slower rate than do dry and thin-bodied brews. Don't let this mental exercise intimidate you because absolute precision is not critical, and with a little experience, the calculations become second nature.

Don't Drink Out of a Bottle or Can

You will automatically get a gassy stomach whenever you drink beer directly from a bottle or can. Before the brew goes down your hatch, you have to release some of the carbon dioxide in the beer by pouring it into a glass.

Select the Best Drinking Container

The advantage of clear glass over opaque material such as stoneware is that it allows you to enjoy and judge the hue, bead (rising bubbles) and head of a brew. This is especially true when you have a pale or amber, rather than a dark, beer in front of you.

Stoneware, on the other hand, will keep a beer cooler in a hot environment because it is a slower conductor of heat than glass. Should you be drinking in direct sunlight, the stoneware also filters out solar radiation which would otherwise warm the beer.

Pewter is visually quaint; but, unlike glass and stoneware, it can impart an off-flavor. Pewter tankards are best left hanging from the rafters as decorative features.

The shape of the glassware will affect your olfactory perceptions. I have discovered that tulip-shaped glasses are best because they most efficiently capture and focus the elusive aromas and bouquets emitted by a beer. The brandy snifter is the most ideal of the tulip-shaped glasses, but the wine and champagne varieties are nearly as suitable for judging beers.

Though I love the elegance of the conical pilsner glass and its ability to foster a large beer head, it has a drawback. It does not corral the volatile odorants as well as a closed-in-rim glass such as a snifter. I also like the charm of mugs, steins and tankards, but they share the weakness of Pilsner glasses. So do ordinary tumblers, which have the added disadvantage of being visually unexciting.

Use Sparkling Clean Glasses

The slightest grease smudge or thinnest oily or fatty film on the interior surface of your glass will keep the head of your beer from growing to its full potential. So will dust and dirt.

Besides being squeaky clean, the glass should be free of foreign odors that it may have acquired, for example, in your cupboard. Unless you know for sure that a glass was recently washed, give it a sniff test.

Wash the glass in hot water with detergent rather than soap because the latter leaves a fatty film of residue. If detergent is unavailable, use baking soda.

Once washed, the glass must be thoroughly rinsed with hot water and then air dried. Towels can leave lint and, if they have been used for other chores, grease and off-odors.

Do Not Rinse the Glass with Cold Water

One of the most prevalent myths among casual beer drinkers is that a brew will develop a bigger head if you rinse the glass with cold running water just before you use it. In fact, the opposite occurs, as a simple experiment in your kitchen will demonstrate.

There are two reasons why a knowledgeable bartender may rinse your glass before drawing or pouring your beer. You may be getting one of the first servings from a freshly tapped or particularly gassy keg and the bartender doesn't want to give you an exceptionally large head. Or, your glass may have picked up barroom odors (including stale smoke) as it sat on the shelf. In such a case, a quick rinse would be welcomed despite its stunting effect on the head size.

Decant Certain Beers

Some beers like the lambic and wheat beers will throw a yeast sediment. Unless you decant, the sediment will blend into the beer, giving the brew a cloudy appearance and a yeasty flavor. Some beer drinkers appreciate the result, most do not.

Sedimented bottles of beer need to rest in a vertical position in the refrigerator for a day or two to give any precipitates a chance to settle. Then, the bottle is gingerly removed from the refrigerator and opened.

You decant the beer as you would a bottle of wine except, in this case, you transfer the beverage directly to the drinking glass rather than to a decanter. The sediment is left behind in the bottle and discarded.

Slowly pour the beer into the glass. Ideally, it should be large enough to accommodate all the decanted liquid because you must pour the beer in one steady motion. The sequential act of half pouring the beer, setting the bottle down and then pouring the beer again stirs up the sediment.

If you are decanting the beer into two glasses, arrange the glasses in tandem. Fill the first and then—without righting the bottle—fill the second glass.

Stop pouring the beer the moment the sediment begins to appear in the neck of the bottle. If you decanted properly, you will have sacrificed only 10% of the beer, the portion that remains in the bottle with the sediment.

Peel Away the Foil Wrapper from the Lip of the Bottle

The necks and tops of some beer bottles are sealed with a decorative foil wrapping. Should the beer come in contact with this foil as it is being poured, it will pick up a metallic flavor, the type that produces an unpleasant tooth-coating sensation. Remove the foil completely from the lip area of the bottle before you pour the first drop.

Pour the Beer Correctly

There are two schools of thought about pouring beer from a bottle or can. One faction argues that you should tilt the glass and trickle the brew down its sides. The opponents assert that the beer must be poured straight down the center of a vertically positioned glass, creating a turbulence that will develop a worthy head.

In most circumstances, the down-the-siders are wrong and the down-the-centerers are right. Unless a beer is sufficiently aerated, it will not release enough carbon dioxide or aromatics.

How, then, did the down-the-side approach become popular in America? I suspect the major reason is that people see bartenders do it when their kegs are very gassy or have just been tapped. Another influence is television commercials. Advertising agencies choose the down-the-side technique because it looks more elegant than pouring it plop-plop style down the middle of the glass. (The actors do not risk getting gaseous bellies because, as you probably have noticed, the TV spots never show the performers quaffing the brew, an act that is proscribed by a self-imposed television industry code.)

There are four circumstances when it makes sense to violate the down-the-center rule. The first is when you are dealing with a bottle or can of beer that, for one reason or another, has been severely agitated. If you see an abnormally large head forming, immediately switch over to the down-the-side approach.

The second is when the altitude is lofty, as is the case in the mile-high city of Denver. (This and other head-size determinants are discussed on page 27.)

The third situation that calls for breaking the rule is when you are serving a wheat beer. The high protein content of wheat beers fosters the development of huge heads. For these brews, I recommend a half-and-half approach: start off with the down-the-side tactic and finish with the down-the-middle method.

The final exception to the down-the-middle dictum is when drawing beer from a keg that has been freshly tapped or over-pressurized. In either case, the down-the-side approach may be your only practical method of preventing a behemoth head.

Whether you are using the down-the-middle or down-the-side approach, there is a proper pace and rhythm to pouring beer. The pace can be described as slow and steady and the rhythm as smooth and graceful. This art can be best learned by watching a seasoned bartender.

The quantity you pour into the glass will depend on your goal. If you want to judge the beer, leave airspace in the glass for collecting the volatile odorants. If you simply want to lean back and enjoy the brew, pour it until it has a sizable collar, the portion of the head that rises above the rim of the glass. The maximum possible height of this collar is greater for quality beers than it is for ordinary brews because they have denser, firmer heads.

Sip, Don't Quaff, Quality Beers

Fine brews are savored slowly; ordinary ones are swigged absentmindedly. (According to the *Guinness Book of World Records*, someone downed a liter in 1.3 seconds. That's a mark I would be embarrassed to hold.)

TAPPING A KEG

I vividly recall my old college fraternity keg parties. The beer we drank was often two-thirds foam because neither my Sigma Alpha Epsilon brothers nor I knew how to tap a keg properly. On one occasion, the brew gushed out of the bung hole with such ferocity that we literally had the biggest beer blast on campus. Looking back, I can see we always made four basic mistakes:

We handled the keg roughly. Since the keg was made of heavy duty aluminum, we didn't see any need to treat our burden like a ripe tomato. Typically, several of us would jerk the keg off the distributor's loading platform, unceremoniously dump it into the trunk of my car, drive to the party at breakneck speed over a pothole-ridden road and then, with all the machismo we could muster, mightily chuck the weighty keg onto the serving table. This performance is not uncommon.

We didn't allow the keg to rest. Even if we had handled the keg with kid gloves, it would still have needed to rest so that the extra built-up pressure could settle back into the beer. A gently treated keg needs a respite of one to several hours. An abused keg, like the one described in the previous paragraph, requires a full 24 hours.

We didn't keep the keg cold enough. When you pick up the keg from the distributor, it is properly cold—35° to 45°F. Keg beer must be kept within this temperature range because it is usually unpasteurized and, therefore, very perishable. Since we didn't keep it on ice when we transported it to the fraternity party, its temperature rose. We also did not half-bury it in a tub of ice on the serving table. Consequently, the temperature of the lager must have soared above 60°F, high enough to guarantee excessively foamy beer for one and all.

We overpressurized the keg. Immediately upon tapping the keg, we started working the hand pump. Result: too much pressure inside the keg.

Should you ever consider throwing a keg party, here are a few extra pointers that can spell the difference between a successful and a ruined party.

If your neighborhood store cannot order the right keg for you, look under the "beer" listing in the *Yellow Pages* for retailers and distributors who sell kegs. Be forewarned that a filled half-keg weighs about 125 pounds. Since most outlets will not deliver, bring muscle power.

Draft beer is sold in two basic sizes: quarter-keg and half-keg. (Those cute, 5-liter keglike containers displayed on retail shelves are really oversized beer cans, not kegs.) A quarter-keg yields seventy five to one hundred 12-ounce cups, depending on how proficiently you tap the brew. This is the equivalent of three to four cases and will satisfy fifteen to thirty thirsty partygoers. Double the above numbers for the half-keg size.

Which are better, wooden barrels or metal kegs? Wooden barrels are kinder to beer, but since wooden barrels have become practically extinct in this country, the issue may be academic.

Most keg beers need to be pressurized by means of a hand pump, compressed air or a carbon dioxide cartridge. The cartridges save work but impart a gassy mouthfeel. (In the past, beer was drawn off by its own natural pressure, but those days are virtually gone in America.)

The same brand of beer costs approximately 10% to 20% less in the keg than in the bottle. This saving becomes nonexistent if the keg is not tapped properly or if all the beer is not consumed.

Buy the best quality keg beer that you can afford. The extra 25 cents per glass ($25 per quarter-keg) for a brand like Dortmunder Union is a sound investment as far as your tastebuds are concerned.

You will be asked to leave a deposit on the keg and, most likely, on the tapping equipment as well. Be sure to verify that you are being given the spigot and pump that match your particular keg—there are many incompatible styles.

Don't assume that the spigot and pump have been hygienically cleaned. Wash them with detergent (not soap) in hot water as soon as you get home. Then rinse the components thoroughly in hot water and let them air dry.

To tap a keg, you normally insert the pump in the topmost of the two sealed holes and the spigot into the lower one. Some kegs have a combination pump and spigot apparatus; in this case there will be only one hole to tap. Since different keg models have their idiosyncrasies, ask the supplier for verbal or written instructions.

Be prepared to discard the first half pitcher or two that you draw. It's inevitable that this initial outpouring will be excessively foamy unless you were sold a keg of flat beer.

Resist the temptation to increase the pressure in the keg until the beer flow has appreciably slackened. Stop pumping the moment a strong flow resumes.

Don't let the complications of serving a keg deter you from bringing one home for your next party. Not only does keg beer cost less on a per glass basis, it is almost always fresher than bottled or canned brew. As a bonus, a keg lends a festive air to a party.

JUDGING A BAR

Quality standards vary markedly from bar to bar. Though some owners and bartenders know how to select, store and serve beer, many do not. Whenever you visit a bar for the first time, ask yourself these questions.

Are the barroom and restroom clean? If you are contemplating ordering draft beer, pay extra attention to the sanitary conditions in the public rooms. Draft beer is susceptible to contamination by bacteria that aggressively multiply in dark, dirty keg-storage areas and in the pipes that connect those kegs with the serving spigots. Beer so tainted will become sour and, eventually, unwholesome. Establishments that are visibly unconscientious about hygiene will probably not be concerned about cleaning their hidden storage areas and beer pipes on a regular basis. Caveat emptor.

Does the bartender dip the tip of the spigot into the beer when refilling a glass? This is unhygienic because germs from someone else's dirty glass will be transferred to the spigot and eventually to your glass.

Are the glasses sparkling clean? Try to examine the glasses parked on the shelf behind the bar or hung on pegs on an overhead beam. If they are not sparkling clean, your beer will have a stunted head. If they are dirty (as is sometimes the case), you might end up with dysentery.

Does your glass smell? Regrettably, the glasses in most bars smell of dishwasher disinfectants, detergents, smoke or varnish from the shelves. Since the malodorants will negatively affect the quality of your beer, it is wise to sniff the glass before you pour the beer. (If the bartender has poured it for you, there is little you can do.) Should your glass flunk the scent test, ask for an odor-free replacement or for your glass to be rinsed.

Does the bar offer draft beer? A brand of beer normally has much more character in the draft than in bottled or canned form. Reason: draft beer is usually not pasteurized or microfiltered—or, at least, not to the same degree that bottled or canned beer typically is.

Bars, however, shouldn't offer a broader array of draft beers than they can sell within several days' time. Draft beer is significantly more perishable than bottled or canned brew.

Is your draft beer flat? There is no excuse for a flat draft beer—one lacking in sufficient carbonation. The possible causes are several. Your beer may have been one of the last to be drawn from a keg—perhaps one that has been sitting around for a long time. (Honorable bartenders discard these bottom-of-the-barrel remnants.) Some of the beer's effervescence may have prematurely escaped because of a drop in the pressure in the keg. This could result, for instance, when a bartender doesn't maintain proper keg pressure or when there is a leak in the keg or piping. Competent bartenders are alert to these possibilities.

Is the draft beer too fizzy? As with flat beer, you shouldn't be happy about a gassy beer. Sometimes the blame for excessive carbonation does not rest upon the brewer's shoulders. Just the other day I crossed-tasted a Heineken in the bottle with a Heineken on draft and found the normally better draft version to be inferior because it had picked up a gassy bite caused by the excessive use of a carbon dioxide cartridge to pressurize the keg. Gassiness also results when the bar doesn't let a freshly delivered keg rest for a day before it is tapped, when it serves you the initial outpourings of a newly tapped keg (if a beer is too foamy, a conscientious bartender discards it), when the keg and pipes are not kept sufficiently cold—or when the pipes are dented or partially clogged.

Is the beer served too cold? I have tested the serving temperature of beers in hundreds of bars and restaurants from Maine to California. In most cases the serving temperature was too low. (For recommended serving temperatures see page 10.)

Is the beer served in frosted mugs? Frosted mugs may impress the casual beer drinker, but an icy coating prevents you from judging and enjoying the visual properties of the translucent brew inside. Moreover, since the beer served in frosted mugs is usually too cold to begin with, these mugs don't allow the brews to warm up to a proper serving temperature.

A growing number of bars frost their mugs with automatic frosting devices. Unfortunately, the chemicals used in this process give the glass an unpleasant odor.

Is the bartender arrogantly ignorant? As your knowledge of beer grows, you will become aware of some bartenders convinced that they know more about beer than they really do. I guess this is sort of an occupational hazard. Those bartenders think that the years they've spent behind the polished oak plank automatically confer expertise. Should you dare to suggest anything that conflicts with their accumulated "knowledge" they become indignant. They may refuse to take back an obviously skunky beer because they are unaware of the concept of skunkiness. They may insist that your beer is not flat because by their standards it is not. There is little you can do in these no-win situations except take your business elsewhere.

HOW TO JUDGE THE BEER IN YOUR HAND

BEER EVALUATION: AN OVERVIEW

Could you distinguish your favorite brand of beer from similar ones in a blind tasting? According to informal research that I have conducted across the country, few loyal beer drinkers can. One reason is that mass-marketed American beers are so much alike that differentiating between them is almost as difficult as separating ping pong balls by size, color and weight. A more significant reason is that few beer drinkers have learned the art of judging beers.

However, almost anyone can acquire the skills. All it takes is knowledgeable guidance and thoughtful practice.

Part Two, "How to Judge the Beer in Your Hand," gives you this guidance by teaching you how to evaluate beers via the tried-and-proven five-sequential-step method. I'm sure you will be amazed at how quickly this system enables you to detect an incredible variety of strengths and faults that dwell in beer. You will also acquire the ability to rate beers on a score sheet, as professionals do.

While my book provides the guidance, only you can furnish the practice—the second essential for developing connoisseurship. Since this practice basically entails sampling a wide range of beers from around the globe, I wouldn't exactly call it an unpleasant pursuit.

Remember, the art of judging beer will always be partially subjective. Just as no two people have the same fingerprints, no two individuals have identical sensory capabilities or preferences. As evaluators, we bring to the judging table personal biases and prejudices that somehow rear their ugly heads no matter how hard we try to stifle them. But, there are universal yardsticks that separate, so to speak, the barley from the chaff.

THE FIVE SEQUENTIAL STEPS

The art of judging beer is not difficult if you use these five sequential steps:

> Look
> Sniff
> Taste
> Look Again
> Make a Synergistic Assessment

Step One. Look at the Beer (Appearance)

Lift the glass and hold it several inches in front of a well-lit white background such as a hand-held napkin or blank piece of paper. Study the brew. I want you to pay particular attention to four attributes: the size of the rising bubbles, the condition of the head, and the clarity and color of the liquid.

Bubble size. As with champagne, the size of the individual bubbles streaming upward in your beer provides a clue to the quality of the product. If you see small bubbles, you know you have a beer that was naturally carbonated. Large, fast-rising bubbles suggest that the carbonation was artificially injected into the beer. The process—called carbonic injection—requires significantly less brewing and aging time and care than does the traditional natural carbonation method. Soda pop and run-of-the-mill bulk champagne makers also employ this technique.

Suggested Experiment

Compare the size of the bead (the bubbles) in an ordinary lager with those in a high quality one.

Mediocre ingredients or a mistake by the brewer can also create oversized bubbles. Whatever the cause, the large bubbles unpleasantly overwhelm your palate and obscure subtle flavors. These gassy beers have a short-lived head and are apt to make you belch.

Do not confuse the bead with the large bubbles that sometimes cling to the side of the glass. When you see bubbles of this type, your glass isn't perfectly clean.

Head. Quality beers have thick, dense heads. Those of lesser breeds are feeble and loosely knit.

A bleached rather than a creamy or deep tan head on a dark beer suggests that the brewer artifically colored his product.

Properly poured quality beers have lofty heads, typically one and a half to two inches in height. Abundant suds are not automatically a quality indicator, however. Many brewers attempt to fool Mother Nature (and the consumer) by adding chemical foaming agents to beers that would otherwise be almost as flat as an ice hockey rink. You can easily identify these sneaky brews; their foam bubbles are large and short-lived.

A variation of as little as 5°F in the temperature of the beer will markedly affect head size. If the beer is too cold, its head will be smaller and its odor and flavor will be less intense than normally. The reverse occurs if the brew is too warm. (For guidelines for particular styles of beer, see the "Serve Beer at Its Proper Temperature" section starting on page 10.)

Suggested Experiment

Compare two bottles of beer that are identical except that one is served at room and the other at refrigerator temperature. Note the difference in head size, odor and flavor.

Altitude also affects head size. The higher you are above sea level, the bigger the head because there will be less atmospheric pressure bearing down and, therefore, the carbon dioxide gas can more readily escape from the liquid. I once attempted to pour a normal-size head in a beer at 13,000 feet in La Paz, Bolivia. Even though I used the down-the-side approach, the foam-to-liquid ratio was five-to-one. Can you imagine how foamy my beer would have been if I had poured the beer down the middle of the glass?

There is a host of other variables that determine head size. A beer will develop an uncharacteristically large head if you shake the bottle or overpressurize a keg. The same is true if the beer is the first to be drawn from the keg. Because of differences in the shape and smoothness of the container openings, the same brand of beer will have a smaller head when it is poured out of a bottle than a can.

The head size will not reach its full potential if the brew is stored too long, gingerly poured down the side of the glass, or served in a greasy, dusty or watery glass. Ditto if it is one of the last servings from a keg. Another determinant is the distance between the mouth of the bottle and the glass during the pouring.

Clarity. There are four basic terms for describing the degree of clarity of a beer. In descending order of transparency, they are:

> Brilliant
> Clear
> Hazy
> Cloudy

A beer is clear, hazy or cloudy as opposed to brilliant because of minute particles, such as dead yeast cells, suspended in the liquid. For most beers, nonbrilliance is a fault, though there are exceptions. Unfiltered wheat brews, for instance, are by their nature misty. Beers made with 100% barley and flavored liberally with whole hops are also haze prone. Bottle-conditioned ales occasionally throw a sediment which would fog the beer should you jiggle the container.

High-tech American pale lagers like Miller High Life are virtually always brilliant, but not because of any remarkable quality. These products are bright because they are hyper-filtered and made with a large proportion of nonbarley grains such as corn. Should haziness develop in any of these beverages, you know something dreadful occurred after the bottle left the brewery.

There are many causes for an uncharacteristic haze in a beer. The brewer could have unskillfully concocted his product or used an inferior strain of yeast. The beer may have become bacterially contaminated. Perhaps you refrigerated the beer for an excessively long period. Maybe you served the beer too cold. (This "chill haze" starts disappearing as soon as the heat in the room begins to warm the beer.)

Do not confuse haze with condensation. The latter is the film of water that forms on the exterior of the glass when the beer and its glass are cold and the surrounding air is warm and moist. In order to judge the clarity and color of the beer effectively, you must wipe this wet layer off the entire outer surface of the goblet portion of the glass. I know this task can be frustrating on sultry days when the dew diabolically reappears almost as quickly as it is rubbed away.

It is not easy to judge the clarity of a dark-hued beer. You can gain some useful information, however, if you hold the beer up to a light and examine the fringe of the liquid.

Color. Focus your attention on two aspects of the beer's color: its particular hue (the position on the chromatic spectrum) and the depth of color. The concept of hue is easy to grasp; think of red, orange, yellow, green, blue, and so on. To understand what is meant by the depth of color, imagine drawing a line with a brown crayon, exerting normal hand pressure, on a white piece of paper, then making a parallel line using heavier pressure. The two lines will have the same hue (brown) but different depths of color.

Depths of color in a beer cover a broad field, from pale to opaque. Beer hues range from ethereal golden to brownish black. Sometimes the basic hues are emerald or ruby tinged.

Hue should be appropriate to the particular beer style or substyle. International pale lagers are customarily delicately golden, sometimes with a trace of green. An Irish stout is usually chocolate brown. (For the orthodox colors of other beer types, see Part Six, "How Beer is Classified," starting on page 215.)

The brewer has various ways to darken his product. The time-honored and preferred method among quality producers is to caramelize the barley or barley malt by roasting it—the darker the roast, the deeper-hued the brew. Nowadays, many cost-cutting brewers literally dye their beverage with nonbarley coloring agents.

Step Two. Sniff the Beer (Aroma/Bouquet)

Because your goal is to evaluate the beer, do not completely fill the glass. You should leave at least a couple of inches between the rim and the top of the head in order to provide sufficient airspace within the glass for collecting the escaping odorants.

I find that the ideal glass for judging a beer is tulip shaped. Its upper curve helps trap the volatile molecules. Of the tulip-shaped glasses, the brandy snifter is best for serious tastings. (See "Select the Best Drinking Container," p.12.)

Suggested Experiment

Half fill a straight-sided tumbler and a tulip-shaped glass with the identical beer. Notice how many more odor subtleties you can detect in the tulip-shaped glass.

Place your nose inside the glass. Inhale sharply and deeply. Concentrate on the smell of the beer. Closing your eyes helps.

The first sniff is all important because your olfactory receptors start becoming temporarily desensitized to specific odors a moment or two after they first encounter them. You know how little time it takes after you enter a cheese shop for the smell of the cheese to start losing its intensity. Once this sensory fatigue sets in, you will have to give your receptors a vacation from the odoriferous molecules for at least several minutes if they are to regain their former capabilities. Since that waiting period is impractical for most beer-tasting exercises, you will likely have to compromise. A ten second pause, though brief, is better than no wait at all.

A genteel whiff, the type you would normally use when evaluating a wine, doesn't work for beer. Contrary to popular notion, most of the distinguishing odorants in a beer are less intense than those in a typical wine.

What should your olfactory sensory mechanism be searching for? The answer is the specific scents of malt, hops, yeast and esters. You will also be trying to detect defects such as skunkiness and oxidation.

The scent of the barley malt (the germinated grain) should be clean and fresh. The more the malt has been roasted, the sweeter and more intense the fragrance will be.

Suggested Experiment

To teach yourself to recognize the characteristic scent and flavor of malt, sample a dark, Munich-style beer. The malt

character stands out because a relatively small quantity of hops is used. Alternatively, munch on a few germinated barley grains (available from home brewing supply houses).

The smell of other leading brewing grains like rice, corn and wheat are less detectable because their odorants have less character and intensity. But, these grains (and particularly corn) give off a telltale odor that is best described as "grainy." The lesser the brew, the more obvious and unappealing this odor will be.

Hop aroma is a tonic; it increases your appetite for both brew and food. Its pleasing bitter note also adds liveliness to the beverage and helps balance the natural sweet nose of the malt.

Suggested Experiment

To learn to identify the hop aroma and flavor, drink a well-hopped beer such as Bass Ale. Conducting this experiment simultaneously with the previous one on maltiness is especially enlightening.

Yeasty aroma should not be noticeable except in certain cases, as with bottle-conditioned ales. Yeastiness is a flaw when it obscures delicate scents.

Esters are one of the elusive yet important odorants (and flavors) in beers. It will take a little practice and much concentration on your part to recognize their presence and personalities. These volatile organic compounds are created during the fermentation and maturation processes, and are redolent of certain fruits, flowers and vegetables: apples, apricots, artichoke leaves, bananas, black and red currants, blackberries, blueberries, carrots, cherries, corn, cranberries, figs, grapefruits, lemons, melons, onions, oranges, peaches, pears, pineapples, plums, quinces, raspberries, roses, strawberries, zucchini and other produce.

Most of the fruity, floral and vegetal odorants (and flavors) give beer unique and exciting dimensions. A few of these estery stimuli, such as the bananalike isoamyl acetate chemical, can harm a brew.

Skunkiness is the result of a chemical reaction that occurs when a bottled beer is subjected to prolonged exposure to natural or fluorescent light. Tinted glass slows down but does not prevent the reaction that takes place in the bottle.

The first odor you recognize when you open a skunky beer can best be described as being halfway between that of a threatened skunk and overcooked cabbage. Eventually, this initial scent fades and a new offensive odor reminiscent of a wet dog and wet cardboard dominates.

A skunky beer markedly loses its freshness and fruitiness, and has unbalanced acidity. Though the brew may still be effervescent, it will taste dead.

Suggested Experiment

The best way to learn exactly what skunkiness denotes is to buy two identical bottles of beer, storing one on a sunlit window sill and the other in a cool dark closet. In one week, chill, open and compare the beers.

Oxidation imbues a beer with an objectionable leathery or pungent, burnt Madeira-like nose. It is the result of a chemical reaction that takes place when an excessive quantity of oxygen comes in contact with beer for a lengthy period. Perhaps the bottle left the brewery with too much airspace (ullage) or the container or its lid was not hermetically sealed.

Beers stored too long in a hot environment acquire "baked" defects. They exhibit sulfuric (the smell of rotten eggs or a just struck match) and wet cardboard scents. Increased bitterness is also noticeable.

Suggested Experiment

Buy two identical beers. Store one in a cool dark closet and the other in an unlit gas oven. (The pilot light should heat the oven to a temperature in the 100° to 120°F range.) After three days, chill, open and cross-taste the beers.

Other identifiable off-scents exist. These include sour, grassy, stale, musty and moldy odors. (See the "Tasting Terms" chapter beginning on page 53 for definitions of these and other scents.)

Step Three. Taste the Beer (Flavor)

When we speak of the taste step, we are really talking about assessing flavor, which is taste and then some. Taste in the limited sense of that term involves only the tastebuds, of which we have four primary types: those that are sensitive to sweet, salty, sour or bitter substances. Though these tastebuds are distributed throughout most of your mouth, they are concentrated on the top and sides of your tongue. Most of the sweet receptors are bunched at the tip, the salty and sour on the front sides, and the bitter receptors toward the rear of your tongue.

Flavor, an oft-misunderstood term, embraces more than these four basic tastes. It also encompasses the odor that reaches your olfactory receptors from the inside of your mouth as opposed to through your nose. As the beer rolls around in your mouth, aromatic fumes are released and travel upward through a passageway linking the rear roof of your mouth with the nasal chamber. This hidden corridor is called the nasal pharyngeal. Most people are unaware of its existence and, consequently, they ascribe to taste what is really odor.

Flavor also embodies mouthfeel, the umbrella descriptive for sensations like touch, pain, temperature, pressure and movement. These stimuli are detected by receptors other than those that report tastes and odors.

You experience the flavor of a sip of beer in three distinct phases:

Foretaste
Midtaste
Aftertaste

Foretaste (or antetaste) is the brief initial sensation imparted by the beer when it first touches your lips and enters your mouth. You are more apt to detect sweetness than bitterness in this phase because your sweet tastebuds have a tactical advantage: they are deployed up front while the bitter ones are entrenched in the rear.

A split second later you begin to sense the midtaste, which can last a second or two. The flavor profile during this phase is normally more complex and profound than that of the foretaste. Some inferior beers have sparse (or hollow) midtastes.

Aftertaste is a rewarding, although definitely the most over-looked, phase of drinking quality beers. The finish, as aftertaste is also known, is the lingering flavor that commences after you have swirled the beer around in your mouth for a second or two, or once the beer goes down your throat. It lasts for up to several seconds thereafter. This finish will be harsh, aggressive, tannic, sour or cloying—and usually (we hope) short-lived—in poorly made brews. Superb beers boast finishes that are smooth, elegant, complex and long-lived. A worthy finish is a lingering adieu that prolongs the pleasure of each sip.

With these concepts in mind, let's proceed to the process of judging the flavor of a beer. Take a generous sip and move the beverage around your mouth as if you were trying to chew the fluid. Be sure that the sample comes in contact with all the surface areas of your tongue and oral cavity, including the zone in the back of your mouth. You want to give every sensory receptor a chance to report its findings to your brain.

To increase the quantity of odorants that reach your olfactory receptors through the passageway linking your oral cavity and nasal chamber, suck in some air through your lips. This mini jet stream increases the perceived flavor of the beer because it helps release the volatile molecules from the liquid and wafts them to the rear of your mouth.

Barley malt or, sometimes, adjuncts such as corn or rice provide the foundation of the flavor in a beer. As with the aroma, this flavor should be clean and fresh.

Flavor intensity in nonhoppy beers is mainly a function of the type of grain used (barley is more flavorful than wheat, corn or rice) and how much the grain or malt has been roasted. Thus, you could reason that the primary grain in Miller's Lite is neither barley nor roasted while that in Guinness Stout is barley and substantially roasted.

The flavor of the malt in beer ranges from weak to strong. Budweiser Light, which is brewed with a large proportion of barley malt substitutes, is an example of the weak variety. Heineken typifies the moderate and Guinness Stout the strong ilk. You will find gourmet beers in both the moderate and strong, but never in the weak classification.

Though beers made with 100% barley malt are generally more gustatorily rewarding than those made partially or totally with adjuncts, there are exceptions. I would rather have a skillfully brewed adjunct-based beer than an ineptly brewed all-barley beer. When eating delicately deep-fried tempura specialties, I would prefer the crispness and moderate strength of flavor of the part-rice Kirin beer to an assertive, full-bodied brew. On hot days, the characteristic high acidity of the part-wheat Berliner Weisse beer can refresh your soul and body.

One of the specific malt flavor components to look for is sweetness. Traditionally, this quality is imparted by the barley malt. If the malt is roasted, this sweetness takes on caramel overtones. The more the malt is roasted the more this caramelized odor and flavor develop.

Quality dark beers possess a tempting caramelized malt flavor. Humdrum brands often substitute nonmaltose caramelized sugars such as corn syrup (dextrose) or beet or cane sugar (sucrose). Rather than exhibiting a pleasing malty sweetness, these brands display a crude sugary sweetness reminiscent of caramel candy or molasses.

There are four basic degrees of sweetness in a beer. In reverse order of sweetness, they are (with examples):

Dry (Grolsch)
Medium-dry (Molson's Canadian)
Medium-sweet (Dos Equis)
Sweet (Mackeson Stout)

The first term on the list obviously doesn't mean free from moisture. Dry in the beer and wine taster's lingo denotes the opposite of sweet. Don't ask me why.

The perceived degree of sweetness in a beer can can be deceiving. High acidity partially masks sweetness, and vice versa.

Some beer judges automatically give a low rating to any beer that isn't dry. This isn't fair. To be objective, you must evaluate the sweetness of a beer in keeping with its particular style.

Hops, too, play a major flavoring role in many beers. Besides offsetting the sweet malt flavor, the bitterness of hops acts as an appetite stimulant. Hops also contribute an herbaceous flavor which, to some palates, is an acquired taste.

Don't be surprised if the hops you smelled in Step Two bear scant sensory correlation to the hops you taste. Brewers use both flavor and finishing hops. The first kind is added at the onset and the second type—the aromatics—near the end of the brewing phase.

Identifying the particular type of hops used in a beer is challenging, even for a seasoned brewmaster. There are numerous varieties of hops, and brewers often use a blend of them to create a house character. You shouldn't, however, have much trouble in learning the distinctive flavor of Bohemian Saaz hops (try a Pilsner Urquell) or Brewer's Gold (sample a Ballantine Pale Ale).

Yeastiness is an acceptable flavor in a few beers such as bottle-conditioned ales. Some beer drinkers even seem to like it for its own sake; I've seen Belgians adding a smidgen of yeast to their beer in the pub. In general, however, yeast flavor more pronounced than a background note indicates a botched product.

Body (thickness) is a mouthfeel sensory perception and ranges from thin- to full-bodied. Thin (watery) is never desirable. Medium or full can be, depending on the style of the beer. Within the thin-bodied category are the American light beers. Mass-marketed standard American beers fall in the light-to-medium bracket. Quality pale lagers illustrate the medium-bodied, dark ales the medium-to-full-bodied, and stouts the full-bodied categories.

The perceived thickness of a brew is affected by many factors. Any beers will appear thicker to your senses if the brewer increases the grain-to-water ratio, the alcoholic content or the sweetness. An increase in acidity or serving temperature creates the opposite result.

Esters, those compounds we discussed in Step Two, can enrich the flavor of beer. Most fruity esters please the palate. Some, such as the bananalike, tend to debase the brew.

Before we conclude this section on evaluating the flavor of beer, let's examine the negative indicators that are described as improperly carbonated, highly acidic, astringent, winy, sour, metallic, medicinal, salty and cooked.

Carbonation, a mouthfeel sensation, prickles your mouth and nose. Without these carbon dioxide bubbles, the brew would be flat and lifeless. Too much of it and the beer would be gassy, like soda pop. Excess effervescence also assaults the palate, hampering the effectiveness of your tastebuds and other sensors.

Acid in beer is essential. It adds liveliness, counters flavor flatness and, in combination with hops, helps balance the sweetness of the malted grain. There comes a point, though, when the level of acidity gets out of hand, even in the case of high-acid wheat beers. And there is one type of acidity you never want in a beer, even in minute quantities. I'm talking about acetic acid, the vinegar compound created when certain airborne bacteria attack the beverage.

Astringent substances, such as tannins in beer, taste rough and coarse. They also have a mouth-coating quality and, like acids, can make us pucker because they constrict tissues in the mouth. A modicum of this sensory stimulus produces a gratifying sensation, but outright astringency is always a gustatory offense.

Winy, vinous, heady and spirited are terms used to describe a high alcohol content. One of the drawbacks to winy beers is that the flavor of the alcohol overwhelms many of the other flavors. Abundant alcohol, as most of us discovered as teenagers, also has a propensity for making us tipsy. Alcohol content manifests itself by creating warming, mouth-filling and, to a lesser degree, biting sensations in your mouth. It is less apparent in sweet, full-flavored beers than it is in dry, bland ones.

A metallic taste can be off-putting. It can be detected with a mouthfeel sensory mechanism called the sense of common chemical. It is usually picked up by the beer when the embryonic beverage comes in contact with metal pipes and vessels during the brewing and maturation periods. Long-stored beer in an aluminum keg or can also picks up a metallic taste. A bottle cap also imparts this defect, but to a lesser degree. (*Note*: Some varieties of hops have an obvious metallic flavor, but this is not a negative attribute unless it is assertive.)

Medicinal-flavored beers smack of old-fashioned pharmaceutical concoctions or cough drops. Another example is the taste of household disinfectants.

Salt is one of the minerals found in hard water. Its taste—up to its threshold of perception—is essential for any quality beer. Obvious salinity is a flaw.

Cooked flavor is reminiscent of canned mik and, if you have a trained palate, ultra-pasteurized cream. The act of pasteurization—heating the product to a high temperature to kill bacteria in order to extend shelf life—produces the cooked flavor. Well-pasteurized beers artlessly display this defect. Those that are only moderately pasteurized may or may not, hinging on the brewer's skill. Unpasteurized beers never will.

You will find other flavor descriptions in the "Tasting Terms" chapter in Part Three, "Polishing Your Beer-Judging Lingo."

Balance is the final assessment you make in both the midtaste and aftertaste phases. A beer is balanced only if the individual flavor components are in harmony with each other—the bitterness of the hops, for example, should offset the sweetness of the malt, and vice versa. No element should overpower another unless that quality is characteristic of the beer's style. The proper degree of balance varies from beer style to beer style. You should detect prominent maltiness in an Irish stout but not in a traditional Bremener-Hamburger pale lager.

Over the entire flavor-detecting process in Step Three, you must be on the lookout for possible external influences that could alter your perceptions. Any beer will taste better if you are fervently thirsty, especially on a hot day. I recall raving about a beer on a scorching afternoon in Timbuktu on the edge of the Sahara desert only to find the same brand unexciting when I tasted it several days later in a cooler locale.

Certain everyday substances can also be enemies. Piping hot coffee, tea or cocoa can scald your tastebuds to such a degree that it will take a day or two for them to recover fully. Breath mint, toothpaste and lipstick may also make beer taste different, as can spicy food consumed shortly before a tasting.

Excessive acid in the mouth impairs taste, too. You won't be able to judge a brew properly if, for example, you've just sipped orange juice. The same is true if you suffer from dental plaque or a high oral bacteria count.

Step Four. Look at the Beer Again (Aftersight)

Beer tasting is distinct from that of wine because it requires the fourth, the "look again," step. Beer perceptibly changes in the short duration it sits in the glass, and this metamorphosis can tell you much about the quality of the brew.

Soon after any beer is poured its head begins to wane. This ebbing cannot be prevented, but in quality beers it occurs more slowly than with ordinary brews. The columns of rising bubbles are longer-lived, too, in better brews.

After you take a sip, some of the gas bubbles of the head cling to the now-exposed inner surface of the glass. This residue is called Brussels lace because it resembles that weblike fabric. It's a good omen if this lace is abundant and ring-shaped. By the time you have finished drinking a quality beer, there will be a stratified structure of concentric lace bands. In most cases, the lace of a low-grade beer will be meager and patternless.

Step Five. Make a Synergistic Assessment

To make a "synergistic assessment," you evaluate how the appearance, scent and flavor of the beer interact. Some beer authorities employ this fifth step; others do not. I do.

My reason is that you cannot treat the individual judging steps as isolated elements. These factors are often interrelated in a gratifying or unsatisfactory manner. In this case, the whole would be greater or less than the sum of its parts.

An example of positive synergy is when the visual, aroma/bouquet, flavor and aftersight components are not only excellent in themselves but also in harmony with each other: the beer entices you into wanting more. Negative synergy can exist when a beer scores high points in Steps One through Four but lacks overall personality and complexity.

Unfortunately, this fifth step can be abused by novice beer judges in nonblind tastings should they use it as a convenient tool to adjust the rating to confirm their prejudices and other preconceived notions. When this happens, the assessment becomes a self-fulfilling prophecy.

RATING SYSTEM AND SHEET

Keep notes. Unless you have total recall, much of what you assess will quickly become buried in the deepest recesses of your mind.

Note taking also forces you to verbalize your sensory perceptions. This mental exercise sharpens your beer-evaluating skills.

There are dozens of beer-rating systems. The bone that I have to pick with some of them is that they focus almost exclusively on negative facets, forgetting the positive ones. They begin with the assumption that the beer has a perfect score and then start subtracting points for defects. Such systems work successfully for brewmasters who are trying to avoid creating a faulty product, but they do not serve the needs of the connoisseur who approaches a beer with a "What's-good-and-bad-about-this-brew?" attitude. This type of beer lover requires a system that simultaneously punishes flaws and rewards excellence.

The most effective rating system I use has a 0-to-20 scale, with the five sequential steps weighted as follows:

Appearance	0 to 4
Aroma/Bouquet	0 to 5
Flavor	0 to 6
Aftersight	0 to 2
Synergistic Assessment	0 to 3

"The Five Sequential Steps" chapter details what you should be evaluating in each step. When rating the appearance, for instance, you would award 0 points if it is horrendous, 1 if poor, 2 if average, 3 if good or 4 if exceptional by worldwide (not American) standards. After granting a rating for each of the five sequential steps, add the numbers and you have the grand total, which can be as high as 20.

Though I've tasted some foreign brews abroad that rated fewer than 4 points, they are not to the best of my knowledge imported into the United States. Neither are you likely to find in America a domestic commercial brew that rates fewer than 4 points.

The zero- and one-star ratings used in this book are the equivalent of scoring 4 to 8 points on the 20 point numerical rating system. I chose to assign zero to those 4 to 8 point brews that were unusually thin and bland, as are most of the American-style light beers. The better 4 to 8 pointers rated one star.

Two stars equate to 9 to 12, three stars to 13 to 16, and four stars to 17 to 20 points. Occasionally I encountered four-star brews with such unusually distinctive qualities that I elected to grant them a fifth star.

Scoring sheets are helpful beer-judging tools. I suggest that you design one to fit your particular needs. Draw and either type or hand-letter your creation on an 8 1/2-by-11 inch sheet of paper, then make photocopies of this original for your use. On the following page is a sample of one of many possible formats for a multibeer scoring sheet. Should you need more space for your remarks, you can cut down on the number of beer entries per page.

If you feel more comfortable with another rating system or sheet, use it. In beers, as in most other endeavors, there are many successful ways to accomplish the same goal. However, should you be in a group tasting where there will be a consensus rating, everyone must use the same system if the results are to be meaningful.

It is also necessary that all the participants be equally stingy with the points they award. If you have never rated a beer on points before, bear in mind that first timers tend to be so generous that an average beer sometimes garners a good or great beer rating.

Remember to judge brews according to their style. Don't take away points from a Kaiserdom Rauchbier, for instance, because you don't appreciate the smoky flavor that is characteristic of Rauchbier.

Should a beer display an imperfection that developed after the product left the brewery, don't rate it. The blame for skunkiness and other post-brewery defects lies with you or the channels of distribution, not the brewer.

								BEER
								appearance (0 to 4)
								aroma/bouquet (0 to 5)
								flavor (0 to 6)
								aftersight (0 to 2)
								synergistic assessment (0 to 3)
								TOTAL POINTS (0 to 20)
								REMARKS

SCORING SHEET

SPECIAL TIPS FOR BEER-TASTING PARTIES

Why not throw a beer-tasting party for your friends? This type of affair is educational, relatively inexpensive and easy to organize. Besides, I can almost guarantee that your guests will have the proverbial barrel of fun.

You will find many tips and insights that are relevant to beer-tasting parties elsewhere in Part Two as well as in Part One, "Buying, Storing and Serving Tips." Here are a few special pointers.

The Beer

Select the beers with a theme in mind, one that provides a learning experience. If your group of tasters is unfamiliar with the range of styles of beers, it is okay to choose a wide but representative spectrum from a pale, dry lager to a dark, sweet stout. If your group is conversant with gourmet beers, then forego this "comparing apples with oranges" approach. You selection should be narrowly focused—all Christmas beers, for instance.

One of the most sharply focused tastings I have participated in occurred in the Philippines in 1978. I had the opportunity to compare different geographic versions of the same San Miguel brand—all pale lagers, but brewed in the Philippines, Hong Kong and Spain. (The local version had appreciably more depth of character and won, hands down.)

You and your friends will learn more about the fine points of beer if you select quality rather than ordinary beers. Gourmet brews have more subtleties to discover and analyze.

Unless it is being done as an object lesson, don't pit ordinary beers against gourmet ones. Such competition makes a mundane product seem more lackluster than it is, and—this may surprise you—also lowers the perceived quality of the gourmet beer. Thus, if you want to make Schlitz taste its worst, compare it with a brew like Pilsner Urquell. But to do justice to a Pilsner Urquell, cross-taste that lager with a Dortmunder Union, not with a Schlitz.

The number of different beers that your tasters can competently judge at your affair is dependent upon their level of expertise and on how much of the brew they swallow. My limit is generally 10 to 15, though this figure decreases if the beers being evaluated are of similar style.

If your participants are unseasoned tasters, their finer perceptions will usually begin to blur after the third or fourth brew (or with the first if they consume the entire bottle). I'm not advocating that you avoid presenting a dozen different brews at a tasting if your guests are beer neophytes. Since they are not expected to be profoundly analytical, little is lost compared to the advantage of their being exposed to a variety of beers.

Buy an ample supply of each beer. Otherwise, there will not be enough brew in each glass for it to reveal all its strengths and weaknesses. I prefer to purchase one 12-ounce bottle of each specimen for each two to three guests—this gives each person a 4- to 6-ounce sampling. In a pinch, you could serve one bottle for every six individuals, but that works out to only 2 ounces per participant.

The Participants

The minimum number of people you need for a beer tasting is one, yourself. You will learn more, however, if you can share opinions with several to a dozen other souls. Much larger groups are generally not educational for novices. Such an affair would more appropriately be called a beer party than a beer-tasting party, because that is what it usually turns out to be.

Though beer-tasting parties need some structure, they shouldn't be stilted. Encourage your guests to use all their senses, including their sense of humor.

For the optimum fun and learning experience, invite people with a similar appreciation and knowledge of beer. If possible, though, have one expert in attendance to serve as a coach.

The Tasting Procedures

The human senses are usually sharpest in the morning during the two hours before lunch, which is when many professional wine tastings are staged. Since your guests probably won't want to be sipping beer in the morning, consider choosing the second best time of the day: the early evening, before dinner. The taste, olfactory and other senses are not as keen during or just after a full meal.

The type of light source makes a difference. Try to avoid fluorescent lighting because it noticeably adulterates the perceived color of a beer. Your best choice is tungsten or incandescent illumination (the standard light bulb). Natural north light, the indirect sunlight that artists prefer for their studios, creates the least color corruption, but it lacks sufficient intensity for judging the clarity, hue and depth of color of a brew.

Tobacco smoking impairs olfactory (as well as taste) receptors. Interestingly, in a smoke-filled room, it is the nonsmoker who is victimized the most. Research studies have shown that second-hand smoke dulls the sensory receptors of nonsmokers more than firsthand smoke zaps those of the smoker.

Tobacco smoke is not the only participant-induced stimulus that can alter odor perceptions. Perfume and after-shave lotion can be culprits, too.

If any of your guests has a cold or a runny nose, discount his or her assessments. They will be able to judge the attributes of a beer about as well as they can evaluate the merits of a new stereo system when they are wearing ear plugs.

A peek at a label can prejudice the judgment of even the best of authorities and can make a novice wise beyond his expertise. This is why blind tastings are sometimes used to evaluate beers.

For a blind tasting, the beer should be poured in another room or, if that is impossible the bottle should be swathed in a concealing material. You could place the bottle inside a paper bag. (Use tape to secure the wrapping to the upper neck of the bottle and keep the bag loose fitting so as to disguise the shape of the bottle which could provide a clue to a savvy eye.) Or, you could loosely wrap the bottle with aluminum foil. (Don't let the foil touch the lip of the bottle or the beer might pick up a metallic taste.) Unfortunately, there is no way to hide the height of the bottle or the color of its rim with the aluminum foil or paper-bag method.

Use a coding system to match the contents in a glass with the appropriate bottle. You could affix corresponding number- or letter-coded self-adhesive labels to the base of the glass and the sides of the bottle. Another system is to tie matching ribbons around the stem of the glass and the neck of the proper bottle.

Once the judging has been completed, the identities of the various beers are disclosed. For me, this is usually a humbling moment.

Each glass used during the tasting should be uniform in size, shape and thickness if the results of the cross-tastings are to be empirically comparable. Ideally, there should be a fresh glass for each person for each type of beer. For serious tastings, use only stemmed glasses—and hold them by their stem, as their designers intended you to do. Never grasp them by their bulbs because that will obscure your view, hinder light penetration and partially tint the beer the color of your flesh. You run the risk of leaving behind some obscuring greasy fingerprints or smudge prints, too.

Glassware selection is not as critical for novice beer tastings. If you don't have enough stemmed glasses, go ahead and use the less-than-ideal glass tumblers and the like, as long as they are absolutely clean and colorless. If you cannot muster the needed quantity of glassware from your cupboard, your neighbor, or a catering or party supply firm, consider buying a supply of the plastic cups sold at your local supermarket. Because they are disposable, they will lighten your post-party cleanup chores.

Pouring consistency is imperative. You have to pour the brew in the identical manner and to the same level each time so that the size of the head is dependent on the beer per se and not on the whim of the pourer.

As in wine tastings, a varied assortment of beer should be served in this order: mild-flavored before strong-flavored; dry before sweet; light-bodied before full-bodied.

Suggested Experiment

Take a sip of pale lager then one of a stout, and then one of the pale lager again. Notice how much blander the pale lager seems the second time around.

Inform your guests that there is a tendency to misassess the first beer tested. Novice beer judges tend to overrate it. In contrast, many seasoned tasters go to the other extreme. In their attempt to make an adjustment for the "first beer bias," they overcompensate.

Remarks made at a tasting can sway the opinion of some guests, particularly if they doubt their proficiency and think highly of the commenter's expertise. Advise participants not to vocalize their opinions until everyone else has had a chance to form his own. By giving the fledgling beer experts in the group a minute or two to draw conclusions independently, you help them improve their beer-judging skills.

Few things are worse than insisting that everyone at a friendly tasting openly express his judgment of a beer, either orally or on paper. Let those who want to share their opinions do so and leave the rest alone. If you are passing out score sheets, let your guests fill them out anonymously if they wish.

Your guests may find it helpful to cleanse their palates between beers so that flavors don't overlap. The best way to purge the mouth of leftover tastants from a previous beer sample is with a small bit of unseasoned white bread or with a sip of room temperature (not icy) tap water. Though salty snacks such as peanuts, pretzels, corn chips and potato chips are customary accompaniments to beer, they desensitize the palate, as do fat-rich items including cheeses and sausages. Keep those goodies under lock and key until after the beers are judged.

If your group is seriously, rather than casually, judging more than a few beers, consider using a spit bucket as wine tasters do. Though some beer authorities claim that these spittoons are superfluous for beer tastings, I disagree. It's a matter of science, not opinion. When beer is swallowed, the liquid ends up in the stomach. The fumes of those beers then rise through your esophagus, producing a false perception of the new beer the taster is currently swirling in his mouth. Since beer is gaseous and table wines are not, it can be reasoned with some justification that a spittoon is even more critical for beer tastings than for wine tastings.

Keeping the alcohol out of your stomach has a second important advantage. Because only a few drops of alcohol reach your stomach, only a Lilliputian quantity of that compound will travel to your brain. Therefore, your senses will not be dulled.

Don't be concerned that the beer won't reach the sensory receptors in the rear of your mouth and upper throat if you don't swallow it. Enough inevitably does if you actively swirl the brew around your oral cavity.

The bucket is normally placed on a table near the tasters. You need not go out and purchase a solid gold Tiffany spittoon. A clean, disposable plastic bucket from your local Southern fried chicken outlet admirably does the trick.

After you have finished judging the beers, you can go back to quaff them to your heart's delight. Headiness and upsurging fumes will no longer be an organoleptic issue.

PART THREE

POLISHING YOUR BEER-JUDGING LINGO

A WORD ABOUT WORDS

Half the battle in judging a beer is knowing the words to describe it. When you are familiar with these terms, you'll know what to look for. You'll also be able to understand what a beer connoisseur means when he says, for example, "the brew is fatty." Equally important, you will be better able to share your opinions with your friends, which is part of the fun of drinking beer.

No one universal beer lexicon will ever exist, because professional tasters and connoisseurs have different needs and perspectives. They do not always use the same argot to describe beer, and my lexicon could not possibly serve the requirements of both the layperson (you) and the brewmaster (the professional who has millions of dollars in potential profit or loss riding on his decisions).

I have discovered that pros utter few metaphors, similes or analogies, preferring shoptalk instead: "Ah, a trimethylamine, anetholelike note!" While lab gab is usually de rigueur for them, it takes a lot of fun out of the game for us nonprofessionals. And where would literature be if a novelist could not pen, "The ale was as invigorating as a crisp, autumn breeze"?

On the other hand, one can go overboard. I heard someone say that a certain beer brand tasted like "an old tennis shoe." If he actually knew the taste of an old tennis shoe, that would be his problem, not mine.

Many a beer snob spits out descriptives, not caring whether the listener grasps the intended meaning. Their attitude reminds me of that of Humpty Dumpty when he advised Alice in *Through the Looking Glass*:

'When I use a word, it means
just what I choose it to mean.'

Beer tasters are sometimes guilty of begging the question. To them, a stout is stoutlike. Still others mumble vague reactions on the order of "it's good" or "I don't like it."

To help you articulate what your palate is experiencing, I have composed for you a list of more than a hundred descriptive terms, the ones you are most likely to hear spoken by crack connoisseurs at serious beer tastings. My lexicon is the most comprehensive of its kind, but it is by no means all-inclusive. To keep the list down to a manageable size, I chose not to define words like "splendid" and "awful" whose meanings are obvious to all.

Neither have I included terms that belong more to the realm of beer scientists and technicians than to that of gourmet circles. If you are interested in learning about descriptives such as trichlorophenol, I suggest that you write the American Society of Brewing Chemists (3340 Pilot Knob Road, St. Paul, Minnesota 55121) and inquire how to obtain a reprint of the article entitled "Beer Flavor Terminology" that appeared in Volume 37, Number 1 of its *ASBC Journal*.

Many of the descriptives in my list apply only to those beers that have developed post-brewery defects. If you have a reasonably fresh product, those negative terms would be inappropriate. If not, some of them may fit the bill for the particular brew you have before you.

I hope you expand my lexicon by writing in your own additions and refinements. But don't be frustrated if some of your attempts to describe a beer prove futile; some beer attributes defy description. They must be seen, smelled and tasted. All the right words in the world couldn't possibly describe their sensory characteristics. You may know what you mean when you say the hops in a Pilsner Urquell are redolent of the Bohemian forests. But no matter how literate you are and how hard you try, you could never express in unequivocal terms that singular scent.

Keep this lexicon handy as a quick reference source. In no time at all, you'll be fluent in the beer connoisseur's tongue.

TASTING TERMS

Acerbic—Describes a bitter, astringent taste in beer. Not as biting as the taste described as ACIDIC.*

Acetic—Displaying a flaw produced by certain airborne bacteria which impart a sharp, vinegary smell and taste to the beer.

Acidic—Exhibiting a biting, sour taste (lemon juice, for example) often produced by citric acid. Many people confuse the word "acidic" with "ACETIC."

Acidulous—Mildly acid, somewhat sour in taste. If stronger, the taste would be described as ACERBIC or ACIDIC.

Acrid—Exceedingly biting or PUNGENT in taste or odor. Can be very irritating.

Adhesive—Demonstrating a tendency to cling or adhere to another substance, particularly tooth, tongue or mouth.

Aftertaste—The flavor that lingers in your mouth after you have swallowed the beer. It can range in duration from quick to lingering. Great beers have a long, pleasing aftertaste, usually measured in durations of seconds. If a low-grade beer has a protracted aftertaste, it will be an unpleasant one.

Aged/To Age—1. Pertaining to the flavor of a beer that has been allowed to fully evolve and mature. The result can reach the ideal or go past that peak. 2. To age: to ripen or mellow in order to cultivate a desired outcome.

Alkaline—Possessing the bitterness and trace of sourness of an alkali (baking soda, for instance).

Alliaceous—Revealing flavors characteristic of the genus *Allium* (chives, garlic, leeks, onions, scallions and shallots). The flavor ranges from the gentle assertiveness of chives to the singular and enduring pungency of garlic.

Ambrosial—"Fit for the gods" and certainly divine to the noses and palates of mere mortals.

*Small capitals indicate that a word is defined elsewhere in this chapter.

53

Appetizing—Capable of arousing gustatory desire, especially through aroma or visual appeal.

Aroma—There is a technical difference between aroma and bouquet. Aroma refers to the natural odors of the ingredients. BOUQUET defines scents that result from the chemical interactions of the ingredients during the production and maturation periods. As time passes, bouquet becomes stronger and more complex while the aroma diminishes in intensity.

Aromatic—1. Possessing an enticing, nose-tingling scent. 2. A substance with essential oils that surrenders a fragrance.

Assertive—Having a bold quality that is instantly apparent.

Astringent—Harsh, severe, dry, mouth-puckering. The MOUTHFEEL sensation one experiences, for instance, when eating an unripe persimmon.

Austere—Displaying a rather severe, uncomplex taste that is quite HOPPY, ACIDIC or TANNIC.

Bad—1. Unfit to be consumed. Unpalatable. Spoiled. Unsound. 2. Unsatisfactory. Inferior.

Baked—Exhibiting objectionable SULPHURIC and WET CARDBOARD odors and a developed bitter flavor caused by overlong storage in a hot environment.

Balanced—Said of a beer whose sensory components such as alcohol, acidity, sweetness, bitterness, fruitiness and tannin are in harmony with one another.

Bead—1. A bubble of carbonated dioxide gas that rises in a glass of beer. "Small" or "large" refers to a bead's relative diameter. 2. Collectively, the rising columns of bubbles.

Beefy/Meaty—1. Having a bouillon cube odor and taste. 2. A chewy MOUTHFEEL sensation.

Beery—Displaying a smell reminiscent of a room filled with empty bottles of cheap beer the morning after an all-night party.

Biting—Jolting, stinging or startling the mouth's pain receptors with a short caustic sensation.

Bitter—Sharp or biting in taste. Though disagreeable in large doses, a moderate level of the right type of bitterness gives beer a refreshing lift and helps balance the sweetness of the malt. The primary source is usually hops, but roasted grain or malt, as well as inept brewing, can also contribute bitterness.

Bland—Mild, dull, without distinction. Drinkable but characterless.

Body—The thickness of beer as perceived by the sensory receptors in your mouth. The consistency can be thin-, medium- or full-bodied.

Bouquet—See AROMA.

Bready—Redolent of freshly baked bread. YEASTY.

Breed—The unmistakable qualities of class in a beer. Such beers come from brewers who have proven their superiority over a period of decades, if not centuries.

Bright—A synonym for BRILLIANT.

Brilliant—Crystal clear except for the hue and depth of color.

Briny/Brackish—When a liquid or beer is very salty, it is described as briny. When the salinity is outright unpalatable, the term brackish is usually used.

Brisk—Having a fresh, spirited flavor or an animated EFFERVESCENCE.

Burnt—Manifesting the smell, flavor or discoloration of grain or malt that is roasted beyond the scorched point.

Buttery—Smelling or tasting of butter, which is usually unwanted in beer.

Caprylic/Goaty/Hircine—Smelling or tasting like a goat.

Caramelized—Possessing the deep amber color or the sweet, toffeelike flavor of burnt maltose, sucrose or other forms of sugar.

Character—A distinct, interesting personality.

Charm—The ability to delight in an uncomplicated sort of way.

Cheesy—Smelling or tasting like cheese.

Chewy—Dense enough to seem somewhat chewable.

Chocolaty—Resembling the flavor of cocoa. In beer, this taste develops from roasting the barley.

Cidery—Smelling or tasting of fermented apple juice. This is usually a defect and should not be confused with an applelike odor or taste, which can be a positive.

Citric—Possessing the sour, puckerish, acidic flavor typical of fruits of the genus *Citrus*: citron, citronella, grapefruit, kumquat, lemon, lime, mandarin, orange (sweet and bitter), pomelo, tangelo and tangerine.

Clean—Pure in taste and fragrance and free of foreign elements. (Think of spring water as compared to tap water, which in most communities has a tainted flavor.)

Clear—Describes a degree of clarity between BRILLIANT and HAZY.

Cloudy—Describes a murkiness caused by minute suspended particles.

Cloying—Wearisomely sweet. Besides being overly mellifluous, the brew lacks sufficient acid and other balancing notes.

Complex—Exhibiting levels of depth that are subtly and richly interwoven. (Think of the difference in the sound produced by an orchestra and the sound of a single instrument.)

Cooked—Evincing an undesirable flavor imparted by the pasteurization process.

Creamy—1. Having a dense, but delicate, frothy head. 2. Exhibiting a rich, smooth texture.

Crisp—Displaying a firm snappy texture with a fresh, clean, sharp taste.

Delicate—Pertaining to flavors and smells with refined, soft-spoken subtlety or elegance. A delicate beer is medium-bodied, never full. (See BODY.)

Distinctive—Possessing a unique personality.

Distinguished—Extraordinary. Superior. A compliment saved for beers with undeniable greatness.

Dry—In terms of taste, dry is the opposite of sweet. A dry beer has a very low RESIDUAL SUGAR level.

Dull—1. Said of a beer that is indistinctive, having little intrigue. 2. A HAZY beer.

Earthy—Reminiscent of the smell of fresh country soil. In a beer, this evocative scent can sometimes be pleasant, but too much earthiness is a flaw.

Edgy—Exhibiting a sharp, unpolished scent or taste.

Effervescent—Capable of releasing visible and audible carbon dioxide gas bubbles from a liquid. Effervescent ranges from the barely noticeable (sprightly or *pétillant*) to the lively and vigorously animated (soda pop). Also called sparkling, fizzy and carbonated.

Elegant—Having well-rounded, first-rate qualities that fit together with the utmost style, grace and simplicity.

Emphemeral—Fleeting, lasting momentarily. This term is particularly applicable for the ESTERY scents in beers.

Estery—Having the scent and flavor of certain volatile organic compounds formed during the beer production and maturation processes. They are redolent of fruits, flowers and vegetables.

Ethereal—Possessing an airy refined texture or an elegant, delicate taste or hue.

Faded—Said of an opened beer that has lost its positive attributes due to prolonged exposure to air. "Died in the glass" is another expression for a beer that has suffered this deterioration.

Fatty—In beer jargon, a fatty brew has a rich, UNCTUOUS, MOUTHFEEL but has insufficient acidity to balance those qualities.

Fecal—Emitting the odor of the excrement of various mammals, including humans.

Fetid—Foul smelling. Malodorous. Stinking. Stenchy. Rank.

Finesse—Revealing distinguished qualities in a low-keyed, unassertive manner.

Finish—Another term for AFTERTASTE.

Flabby—Said of a beer that is not BALANCED because it lacks sufficient acid.

Flat—Undercarbonated; lacking sufficient effervescence.

Flavor—The combined taste, odor and MOUTHFEEL sensation of a beer when it is in your oral cavity.

Flower/Floral—Redolent of flowers in general or in specific, including: chamomile, dandelion, hops, jasmine, lavendar, mimosa, orange, rose, violet and ylang-ylang.

Foreign Flavor—An off-flavor, but not necessarily a bad one. Raspberry syrup added to beer would be an off-flavor to most Americans but not to Berliners.

Foretaste/Antetaste—The brief perception of a taste that precedes the primary or overriding flavor of a food or beverage.

Foul—Offensive and disgusting to the senses and particularly to that of smell.

Fragrant—Exuding a fresh, pleasing, natural scent.

Fruity—Possessing the taste and fragrance of fruit in general or of a specific type of fruit such as pineapple.

Gassy—Overcarbonated, especially with oversized bubbles.

Generous/Expansive—Freely releasing a powerful BOUQUET and/or FLAVOR.

Glittering—Reflecting light with sparkle and brilliance.

Grainy—Displaying the smell or flavor of the cereal grain (especially that of corn, rice and other adjuncts). In beer tasting, this negative attribute does not refer to texture.

Grainy Malt—Exhibiting both a GRAINY and MALTY odor and flavor. Curiously, a few 100% malt brews possess this characteristic.

Grassy—Manisfesting the scent and taste of either dried or freshly scythed grass.

Green Apple—Evincing the pungent odor and taste of acetaldehyde, which is suggestive of raw cooking apples. Oxidation is one cause.

Harsh—An unpleasant or irritating odor or taste.

Haylike—Resembling the smell and taste of dried grass fodder or straw.

Hazy—Describes a degree of clarity halfway between CLEAR and CLOUDY.

Heady—High in alcohol; intoxicating.

Herbaceous/Herby—Tasting or smelling of a basic cooking herb. Specific nuances include: basil, bay leaf, chervil, coriander leaf, dill, marjoram, oregano, parsley, rosemary, sage, savory (summer and winter), tarragon and thyme.

Hoppy—Exhibiting the odor or flavor of hops. They are predominantly bitter, but also display HERBACEOUS and ESTERY overtones.

Hollow—Describes the taste sensation that has a pronounced beginning and ending, but a feeble middle.

Immature—Said of a beer that has not been sufficiently aged in the vat, cask or bottle.

Insipid—Devoid of or meager in taste, odor or character. Unexciting.

Intense—Having a scent or taste that is highly concentrated. This quality can be an asset or an indication of a poorly executed brew.

Lactic—Manisfesting a sour milk odor and flavor. (Think of yogurt or buttermilk.) In beer, it is often caused by bacterial contamination.

Leafy—Emanating the scent of damp, and possibly decomposing, leaves.

Light—1. Pale in color. 2. Thin in consistency. 3. Low in alcohol. 4. Low in calories. 5. All of the above.

Malty—Having the scent or flavor of germinated barley.

Medicinal—Revealing the disagreeable flavor associated with unsweetened medicines and aerosol disinfectants.

Metallic—1. Possessing a tinny finish which comes from the hops. This is acceptable if not excessive. 2. Having an undesirable taste that is picked up from either the can container or from corrosive metal equipment such as pipes.

Midtaste—The phase of the flavor-detecting process that takes place between the FORETASTE and AFTERTASTE. Most flavors are easiest to perceive during this period.

Mineral—Exhibiting the flavor of minerals (not to be confused with METALLIC). The principal source is the water in-gredient, though malt or hops can also pick it up from the soil they grow in. One specific and distinct mineral flavor is salt.

Molasseslike—Similar to CARAMELIZED, but displaying more of the sweet, bitter, burnt notes of the syrupy by-product of cane sugar manufacturing. A definite flaw when pro-nounced.

Moldy—Musty or stale in odor or taste; reminiscent of a damp, wooden cellar.

Mouthcoating—Gives the sensation of a film forming on your tongue, tooth or mouth (can be oily, greasy, dusty, sticky, etc.).

Mouthfeel—The in-the-mouth sensations other than taste. Falling within this term are many types of sensations: pain, size, shape, temperature and moisture content, to name a few.

Muscular—Displaying a firm, strong sensory quality.

Musty—Referring to a repugnant stale or MOLDY odor or flavor.

Nose—The scent of a beer encompassing both AROMA and BOUQUET. A big nose usually refers to a powerful, complex bouquet.

Nose-Filling—Of sufficient aromatic intensity to make a dynamic impact on the olfactory sensory mechanism.

Nutty—Exhibiting a taste or scent that hints of nuts. The term nutty also refers to the flavor of those foods that people generally think of as nuts. (A peanut, for example, is a legume and not a true nut.) Specific nutty nuances include: acorns, almonds, brazil nuts, cashews, chestnuts, coconuts, hazelnuts (or filberts), peanuts, pecans, pine nuts, pistachios and walnuts.

Off—Said of a beer that doesn't exhibit its expected characteristics or level of quality.

Oily—Having the slippery textural and MOUTHCOATING qualities of mineral or vegetable oil.

Over-the-Hill—Beyond its prime. Should have been drunk weeks, if not months beforehand.

Oxidized—Pertaining to a beer that has reacted with the oxygen in the air. Beers that are overexposed to that element darken and develop a leathery or pungent, burnt-Madeira-like odor and taste.

Post-Brewery Defect—A flaw such as being SKUNKY which

develops after the beer has left the responsibility of the brewer. Culprits are shippers, importers, wholesalers, retailers or consumers who mishandle the product.

Powdery/Chalky—Consisting of or containing minute pulverized granules. Sometimes the particles are so fine that they go undetected until they come in contact with the tactile receptors in the mouth.

Powerful—1. Having a strong flavor or smell. 2. High in alcoholic content.

Pungent—Evincing a bold, sharp, tangy and penetrating taste and aroma such as that, for example, of mustard.

Putrid—Having the repulsive odor of decay.

Rancid—Spoiled, with the foul odor and taste of decomposed oils.

Residual Sugar—The unfermented sugar in a brew.

Resinous—Displaying a turpentinelike taste and scent that is undesirable in beer.

Rich—1. Having a delicious abundance of a desirable quality. 2. Smooth, velvety texture. 3. SWEET, but not cloyingly so.

Roasted/Toasted—Exhibiting the odor or flavor of grain or malt that has been surface browned but not BURNT.

Rocky—Describes a head with a dense, bumpy surface.

Rough—Evincing harshness or astringency as the beer is sipped and swallowed.

Rounded—BALANCED; void of crude edges.

Salty/Saline—Having or resembling the taste of sodium chloride, the chemical name for ordinary table salt.

Sapid—Capable of stimulating the gustatory or olfactory receptors in an agreeable manner.

Savory—Revealing a pleasing taste and aroma, usually SPICY or piquant.

Scent—A soft-spoken odor that is characteristic of a particular substance, especially of flowers and fruits.

Scorched—Tasting or smelling somewhere between ROASTED and BURNT.

Severe—Having a harsh and stubborn flavor. Also see AUSTERE.

Sharp—Producing an acute piercing sensation that is usually quick and pointed—and HARSH, BITTER, ACIDIC, SPICY, and/or PUNGENT in tone. Piquant.

Simple—The opposite of COMPLEX.

Skunky—Suggestive of the smell of a skunk, overcooked cabbage or burnt rubber caused by prolonged exposure to sunlight or fluorescent lighting.

Smoky—Tasting or smelling of wood smoke, as with Rauchbier.

Smooth—Produces a pleasant tactile sensation in the mouth and goes down the throat easily.

Soapy—Smellling or tasting like an inexpensive fat-based soap bar.

Solventy—Exhibiting the odor and flavor of acetones. (Think of nail polish remover.)

Sound—Describes a drinkable beer, but not necessarily a quality one.

Sour—In the limited sense, sour means ACETIC, a negative descriptive. Broadly speaking, it simply denotes acidity or tartness, whether the tastant is ACETIC or ACIDIC.

Spicy—Having the taste and aroma of spices in general. Specific nuances include: allspice, anise seed, asafetida, capsicum (chili pepper, etc.), caraway seed, cardamom, cassia, celery seed, cinnamon, clover, coriander seed, cumin, dill seed, fennel seed, ginger, mace, mustard seed, nutmeg, paprika, peppercorn, saffron, and turmeric.

Sprighty—Subtle effervescence. Also known by the French term, *pétillant*.

Stale—No longer fresh. FLAT and INSIPID.

Straightforward—Openly manisfesting its characteristics. Because a straightforward beer has no nuances, it is best drunk without further examination or, for that matter, discussion.

Strong—1. Abundant in one or more distinctive qualities or ingredients. 2. Having a high alcoholic content.

Subtle—Speaking delicately to the senses.

Sulfuric/Sulfurous—Emitting an unmistakable, offensive nose-prickling odor similar to that of rotten eggs, or a just-struck match.

Sweaty—Redolent of human perspiration. When that smell becomes offensive, the descriptives "sweatshirt" and "locker room" are sometimes applied.

Sweet—Tasting of sugar (sucrose, maltose, fructose, etc.) or honey.

Tacky—Having a sticky, adhesive MOUTHFEEL.

Tangy—Sharp, PUNGENT or ZESTY in odor or taste.

Tannic—Produces the ASTRINGENT mouthfeel sensation of tannin.

Tarry—Redolent of a recently laid blacktop road. Tasting of pitch.

Tart—Acid or SOUR, usually in the positive sense.

Taste—Of or pertaining to such gustatory sensations as SWEET, SOUR, SALTY and BITTER.

Texture—The feel of beer in the mouth.

Tingling—Producing a host of minute and usually pleasurable, prickling, stinging sensations in the oral or nasal cavity or on the lips.

Tired—Lacking freshness.

Unctuous—Having a rich, smooth, FATTY or oily mouth-coating character.

Vapid—INSIPID. DULL. Characterless. Zestless. Having lost its flavor.

Vegetal—Exhibiting the AROMA or TASTE of edible nonwoody-stemmed plants, and in particular, vegetables.

Velvety/Silky—Possessiing a rich, smooth TEXTURE.

Vinegary—Smelling or tasting of ACETIC acid.

Vinous/Winy—1. Resembling the odor or flavor of white wine. 2. Noticeable alcoholic content.

Warming—Creating the semblance of increased heat in your mouth by means of the beer's SPICY or alcoholic components.

Watery—Thin-bodied. Diluted beyond desirability.

Weak—Lacking in odor, flavor, color and/or CHARACTER. Having a low level of characteristic ingredients.

Weedy—Having the undesirable flavor of weeds and low-grade herbs.

Wet Cardboard—Demonstrating the off-odor and flavor caused by oxidation, high storage temperatures or overexposure to sunlight or fluorescent lighting.

Wet Dog—Emanating that unmistakable and unappealing smell of the rain-drenched coat of a canine.

Withered—No longer fresh because it has remained in the cask, bottle, can or glass too long.

Woody—Revealing the TASTE or AROMA of wood in general. (Beers can pick up a woody note from storage barrels.)

Yeasty—Smelling of fresh, fermenting or fermented yeast.

Zesty—Lively and piquant.

PART FOUR

HOW DO YOUR FAVORITE BEERS RATE?

WHAT'S IN A RATING?

The number of imported and domestic beers sold in America today is staggering. I discovered over 700 of them during my recent coast-to-coast searches for distinct brands that were offered for sale in at least one retail outlet somewhere in the United States.

Though I've tasted, here and abroad, thousands of other brews, perhaps more than anyone else alive, I did not include them within this book. That would have been a waste of your time because they are either extinct or not imported to this country. What's the point of having thousands of additional ratings if you can't purchase the brands within the fifty states?

Instead, I focused my attention on available brands. And I can guarantee you that this is the most comprehensive listing of those brands ever published.

Sometimes, but not often, you will come across a brand that is not rated in my book. There are several explanations. Perhaps the brand is new. Or, it could be that I purposely omitted it because I was unable to find a specimen without a post-brewery defect. (As I mentioned earlier, it is grossly unfair to punish a brewery for a fault created by the distributor, retailer or consumer.)

You will also not find ratings for brands such as these:

> Champale (in any form)
> Malt Duck (apple or grape)

I consider these products more akin to soft drinks in terms of character (but not alcoholic strength) than to beer. Essentially, they appeal primarily to neophyte beer drinkers—or beer haters—weaned on soda pop.

Neither do I rate near (nonalcoholic) brews. They are not true beers in the traditional sense.

Thomas Hardy Ale is not rated, for a far different reason. This

Dorchester, England brew is superb but its flavor profile varies from year to year. Moreover, this ale is a rarity among beers—you need to age it like a fine wine after you bring it home, and it won't live up to its reputation if consumed before its time. Some vintages require ten to twenty-five years to develop properly. I've tasted one that actually survived fifty years.

I rated microbrewery products only if they were bottled and I could find fresh samples, as was the case for microbreweries like Sierra Nevada and Thousand Oaks. However, some microbrewery beers are sold only by the barrel to local bars "within earshot of the plant's whistle."

In all due respect to the *omitted* microbreweries, allow me to give you the names and locations of some of those that I take seriously so that you may explore their products should you be within their limited marketing areas. This list will probably require constant updating on your part because new ventures are being planned. And, if recent history repeats itself, some microbreweries will disappear quicker than a six-pack at a beach party.

Columbia River Brewing Company
Portland, Oregon

Hale's Ales, Ltd.
Colville, Washington

Hart Brewing
Kalama, Washington

Hillsdale Brewery Company
Hillsdale, Oregon

Independent Ale Brewery (Red Hook Ale)
Seattle, Washington

Kalamazoo Brewing Company
Kalamazoo, Michigan

Küfnerbräu Brewery
Monroe, Washington

Montana Beverage, Ltd.
Helena, Montana

Redwood Brewing Company
Petaluma, California

Reinheitsgebot Brewing Company
Plano, Texas

Roaring Rock Brewing Company
Berkeley, California

Saxton Brewery
Chico, California

Sprecher Brewing Company
Milwaukee, Wisconsin

Stanislaus Brewing Company
Modesto, California

Thomas Kemper Brewing Company
Bainbridge Island, Washington

Widmer Brewing Company
Portland, Oregon

William S. Newman Brewing Company
Albany, New York

Beer shoppers have to be alert for this curve ball: the same brew may be marketed under two names. Differences in state laws usually account for the discrepancy. Take the Luxembourg lager Diekirch. In New York it's labeled "Diekirch Pilsener Beer." However, in California, the law forbids the use of the word "beer" on the label for products with alcoholic contents higher than 4% by volume. The phrase "malt liquor" must be used instead. Because the Diekirch lager exceeds the limit, it is labeled "Diekirch Malt Liquor" in California.

Another source of confusion is a change in label design or wording. Let's say a brewery modifies its brand name from "Flag" to "Uncle Sam's Flag" beer without changing the brewing formula. If the distribution system is inefficient, you might see both brand names in the marketplace for several months.

All the 700 plus beers that I rated were cross-tasted against similar style brands, usually at least twice, sometimes more. Yet, I don't expect you to agree with all my ratings. *Chacun à son goût*—each to his own taste. Even professional beer critics disagree among themselves.

Nevertheless, there are universally recognized standards of excellence that all of us should use. They are outlined in Part Two, "How to Judge the Beer in Your Hand." If you use these criteria, I doubt that our star ratings will differ on more than a small percentage of the beers. Even then, the discrepancy will probably not exceed one star.

I'm the first to admit that my ratings are not infallible. Neither are they permanent. Beers do change. Some brewers will downgrade and others will improve their products. Rest assured, I will continue to monitor these developments closely and will impartially adjust the ratings accordingly in the next edition of this book, as I have done for this updated edition.

KEY

I rate the beers on a zero- to five-star scale:

★ ★ ★ ★ ★
A SUPERB BREW WITH UNUSUALLY DISTINCTIVE QUALITIES
Think of Pilsner Urquell and the American brand, Anchor Steam Beer.

★ ★ ★ ★
A SUPERB BREW
Think of Beck's, Heineken, Kronenbourg and the American brew, Yuengling Porter.

★ ★ ★
A DECENT BREW
Think of Löwenbräu, Michelob and the Canadian import, Molson Ale.

★ ★
SLIGHTLY BETTER THAN THE AMERICAN NORM
Think of Budweiser, Miller and the Mexican import, Carta Blanca.

★
THE AMERICAN NORM
Think of the ordinary American brands and the Australian import, Resch.

THIN AND BLAND
Think of the typical American-style light beer.

You will not see any minus-star ratings in this book, though I have bestowed them on more than a few of the local brews that I've tasted in backwater regions overseas. To receive a minus-star, the beer must be unpalatable—unfit to drink—because of inept brewing. Thanks to modern brewing science, that condition, fortunately, no longer exists for the commercial beers that are sold in America today.

My zero-star rating is conferred on American-style light beers like Miller's Lite that have little going for them except their ability to slake your thirst. If you are mowing the lawn on a scorching July afternoon and someone thrusts one of these brews into your hand, chances are you will find it satisfying. Not all low-calorie beers rate zero stars. A few rate one star and one—Amstel Light—two stars.

Most of the American brands, and a handful of the imported ones, are one-star beers. The greatest volume of beer consumed in America, however, falls within the two-star category, which encompasses Budweiser and Miller High Life, two titans that dominate the marketplace.

Three-star brews should never be shunned, whether they are imported or domestic. Though beer snobs may make sport of Michelob and Löwenbräu because they happen to be produced by the American giants Anheuser-Busch and Miller, my tastebuds say they are decent brews, certainly worthy of three stars. Incidentally, those two brands together outsell all the other three-star as well as the four- and five-star brews that are sold in America.

The beers I want you to pay particular attention to are the four- and five-star brews. These are the gourmet beers, the ones you savor, not quaff. Most are imported but a growing number of them—including Anchor Steam Beer—are American-brewed.

Since my purpose in writing this book is to help you become a beer connoisseur, I have included a succinct description of the sensory characteristics for some of the brews. My goal in these instances is not to give you a detailed analysis, but rather a specific characteristic or two against which you can test your perceptions. This cross-checking will help you sharpen your beer-judging skills. Because of space limitations, I give little or no critique for the individual zero- and one-star brands, preferring instead to let their ratings speak for themselves.

THE RATINGS

★ ★ ★ ★
AASS BOK-BEER (Norway)
Brewed in Drammen. Tan head. Reddish brown hue. Rich, intense, sweet, roasted malt nose. Bittersweet palate and finish. Full-bodied.

★ ★ ★ ★
AASS JULE ØL (Norway)
A Christmas beer. Tea brown liquid topped by a creamy tan head. Rich roasted malt nose. Pleasingly bittersweet malt and hop palate. Full- bodied.

★ ★ ★ ★
AASS NORWEGIAN BEER (Norway)
Also from Drammen. Amber golden. Rich malty nose followed by a hoppy palate.

★ ★ ★ ★
ABBOT ALE (England)
Brewed by Greene, King & Sons in Suffolk. Orange-tinted amber liquid. Tan-cream head. Fruity malt nose. Soft mouth-coating qualities. Heady. Earthy trace in finish.

★ ★ ★
ABC EXTRA STOUT (Malaysia)
Opaque, brown-black hue. Deep chocolaty tan head. Nose and palate have guava fruit undertone. Sweeter than Guinness Extra Stout.

★ ★ ★
ADELSCOTT SMOKED BEER (France)
Produced in Schiltigheim, Alsace. Amber-copper hue. Smokiness is tamer than in German smoked beers (Rauchbiers). Peat smoke attribute is more evident in palate than nose. Sweet backdrop.

★ ★
AEGEAN HELLAS BEER (Greece)
Brewed in Athens. Amber-gold hue. Slightly sweet nose and palate with gassy imprint.

★ ★ ★ ★
AFFLIGEM TRIPEL ABBEY BEER (Belgium)
Brewed in Opwijk near Brussels. Copper-amber color. Large, tannish cream head. Toasty caramelized nose and palate with hint of raisins. Bold headiness—alcoholic content is 8% by volume (6% by weight). Long hop finish.

★ ★
AGUILA (Spain)
An international-style pale lager. Not as full-flavored as the typical European brew.

★ ★ ★
ALBANI (Denmark)
International-style pale lager. Gold hue. Refreshing interplay between malt and hops.

★ ★ ★ ★
ALFA (Holland)
Golden hue. Flowery bouquet. Slight mouth-coating quality. Soft bitter-hop finish.

ALTBAIRISCH DUNKEL (West Germany)
See AYINGER ALBAIRISCH DUNKEL.

★ ★ ★ ★
ALTENMÜNSTER BRAUER BIER (West Germany)
Lustrous golden hue. Fruity aroma. Rich hoppy palate balanced with semisweet maltiness.

★ ★
ALTES BEER (United States)
American-style pale lager with a soft malt underpinning. A product of the G. Heileman Brewing Co.

★ ★
AMARIT LAGER (Thailand)
From Bangkok to you. Hazy, pale golden color. The nose is sweetish and grainy with a tart accent. The flavor is also sweetish and tart with a slightly biting mouthfeel. Bitter aftertaste.

★
AMERICAN BEER (United States)
A Pittsburgh Brewing Company product.

★ ★
AMSTEL LIGHT (Holland)
A low-calorie light beer brewed in Amsterdam. Less sweet and gassy, and more hoppy than the typical low-calorie light beer. (See "Light Beer vs. Light Beer" on page 224.)

★ ★ ★ ★
ANCHOR PORTER (United States)
Brewed in San Francisco by Anchor Brewing Company. Dense, dark tan head tops opaque, brownish black liquid. Rich roasted malt nose. Billowing, bittersweet malt flavor sails into the finish. Hops in evidence. Creamy and full-bodied.

★ ★ ★ ★ ★
ANCHOR STEAM BEER (United States)
Amber beer with an expansive, dense, creamy tan head. The nose

and palate are more malty than hoppy, though both attributes come on strong. Fragrant esters and spicy, bittersweet underpinning. Full, rich body. Superb hoppy finish.

★ ★ ★
ANCHOR WHEAT BEER (United States)
Brewed by Anchor Brewing Company. Fruitier and less tart than German wheat beers. Noticeable gassy mouthfeel. Bitter hop finish.

★ ★ ★ ★
ANCHOR'S "OUR SPECIAL ALE" (United States)
This Christmas beer is brewed once a year and is available only from Thanksgiving to New Year's. Each "vintage" has its own style, but generally they can be described as having an orangy amber hue, fruity hop scent, full sweetish malt flavor, and obvious (perhaps too obvious) bitter hop finish. Both the body and alcoholic content are fairly substantial.

★ ★ ★
ANDEKER LAGER (United States)
Brewed by Pabst. Golden liquid with a cream-colored head. Clean, unassertive nose. Foretaste is hoppy. Mellows to a rich malty palate.

★ ★ ★
ANGEL ALE (England)
The label conspicuously says "steamed brewed" but the product is not made like Anchor Steam Beer. Orange-amber hue. Malty palate with some hops and a background sweetish note.

★ ★ ★
ANGEL BEER (England)
Label boasts "steamed brewed." (See ANGEL ALE entry.) Deep, copper-amber brew with a malty palate. Hops in finish.

★ ★ ★ ★
ARNOLD PILSNER (West Germany)
Brewed in Lauf near Nurnberg. Creamy white head. Brass hued. Malty nose with sweet touches. Hops speak loudest in finish.

★ ★
ASAHI DRAFT BEER (Japan)
Not a genuine draft beer. Brewed in Tokyo. Golden hued. Earthy note to the odor and taste. More flavorful than its competition, Sapporo Draft, but still relatively bland.

★ ★ ★
ASAHI LAGER BEER (Japan)
Brewed in Tokyo. This gold-colored beer has an earthy nose and palate. Short-lived head.

★ ★ ★ ★
ASTRA (West Germany)
Bremener-Hamburger style brew. Golden liquid and pale cream-colored head. Crisp, fruity malt scent and flavor.

★ ★
ATLAS BEER (Greece)
From Athens. Pale golden amber. Nose and palate have citric-sharp notes.

★ ★ ★
AUGSBURGER (United States)
Crafted by the Joseph Huber Brewing Company of Monroe, Wisconsin. Cream-colored head over a deep golden brew. Firm hop, fruity malt nose. Malty palate with hop emphasis.

★ ★ ★
AUGSBURGER BOCK (United States)

Tan head supported by translucent, deep reddish brown liquid. Roasted malt nose. Caramelized malt flavor with balancing hops. Full-bodied.

★ ★ ★
AUGSBURGER DARK (United States)

Translucent orange brown. Malty nose with a bittersweet roasted malt flavor. Hops in background.

★ ★ ★ ★
AUGUSTIJN (Belgium)

Brewed in Ertvelde near Ghent. Deep copper-amber hue. Dense tannish cream head. Toasted malt nose with sweet backdrop. Full-bodied and sensuously chewy. Bitter hops and powdery mouthfeel evident in finish. Heady.

★ ★ ★ ★
AUGUSTINERBRÄU MÜNCHEN DARK (West Germany)

Vatted in Munich. Opaque, reddish brown brew capped with cream-colored head. Obvious roasted malt nose. Long hop bitter aftertaste.

★ ★ ★ ★
AUGUSTINERBRÄU MÜNCHEN LIGHT EXPORT (West Germany)

Not a low-calorie light beer, but a *helles Bier* brewed in Munich. Rich yellow hue. Slightly sweet, fruity nose and palate. More malty than hoppy. Exquisite lace.

★ ★ ★ ★
AUGUSTINERBRÄU MÜNCHEN MAXIMATOR (West Germany)

A reddish tea-colored *Doppelbock*. Sweet roasted-malt nose and palate with a hint of hops in the finish. Medium full-bodied.

★ ★ ★
AUGUST SCHELL PILSENER BEER (United States)
Brewed in New Ulm, Minnesota. Yellow gold. Pale cream head. Malty, somewhat sharp-edged nose and palate. Hoppy finish.

★ ★ ★
AUGUST SCHELL WEISS BEER (United States)
Produced in New Ulm, Minnesota. Sweet-sour profile, especially in aftertaste. Head is smaller and body is thinner than traditional German wheat beers.

★ ★ ★
AUSTRIA GOLD (Austria)
Made in Vienna. Pale gold color. Malty nose. Noticeable citric-tart flavor from midtaste through aftertaste.

★ ★ ★ ★
AYINGER ALTBAIRISCH DUNKEL (West Germany)
Brewed in Aying, southern Bavaria. Opaque, ruby-brown liquid topped with a dense, creamy tan head. Molasses undercurrent in bouquet. Rounded, roasted malt palate with obvious headiness.

★ ★ ★ ★
AYINGER EXPORT-WEISSBIER (West Germany)
Cereal grain base is 60% barley, 40% wheat. Yellow-gold liquid. Large cream-colored head. Sour fruit nose and palate. Suggestions of bananas and salt in finish. Sprightly mouthfeel.

★ ★ ★ ★
AYINGER FEST-MÄRZEN (West Germany)
An amber-hued "March Festival" brew. Sweetish roasted malt nose. Bittersweet palate. Heady.

★ ★ ★ ★
AYINGER JAHRHUNDERT-BIER (West Germany)
This "Century Beer" is produced in Aying southeast of Munich. Pale yellow hue. Toasty malt aroma. Bittersweet palate. Noticeable lace.

★ ★ ★ ★
AYINGER MAIBOCK (West Germany)
A yellow-gold Bavarian-style bock beer. Malty bouquet. Sweetish, mouthfilling character. Detectable potency.

★ ★ ★ ★
AYINGER UR-WEIZEN (West Germany)
Made with 60% barley, 40% wheat. Orange-red amber liquid. Gargantuan tannish cream head. Malt nose and palate with sour-fruit, semi-cidery notes.

★ ★ ★
BALLANTINE INDIA PALE ALE (United States)
A product of the Falstaff Brewing Corporation. Reddish copper hue and fair head. Unmistakable Brewer's Gold hop flavor and finish with woody, metallic undertones. Clinging Belgium lace.

★ ★
BALLANTINE PREMIUM LAGER BEER (United States)
American-style pale lager. Yellow hued. Sweetish grainy nose and palate with a touch of hops.

★ ★
BALLANTINE XXX ALE (United States)
Yellow-gold. Sweetish grainy nose and palate with a hoppy bite.

★ ★ ★ ★
BAMBERGER HOFBRÄU (West Germany)
Golden hue. Ripe, fruity-malt scent and flavor. Aftertaste has touches of sweetness and headiness.

★
BARTELS BEER (United States)
Brewed by The Lion, Inc. in Wilkes-Barre, Pennsylvania.

★ ★ ★ ★
BASS PALE ALE I.P.A. (England)
Brewed in Burton on Trent. Generous and long-lived head and lace. Petite bead. Superb hoppy palate and finish. Hint of smokiness. Mouth-coating quality.

★ ★ ★
BAVARIAN ABBEY (West Germany)
Brewed in Lohr. Brass-tinged liquid topped with pale, creamy head. Hops dominate malt flavor. Noticeable heady finish.

★ ★
BAVARIAN CLUB (United States)
A premium beer produced in Wisconsin by Huber. Golden hued. Sweetish, grainy malt nose and palate, with a moderate bite in the midtaste. Hoppy finish.

★ ★
BAVARIAN PREMIUM BEER (United States)
Produced by D.G. Yuengling & Son of Pottsville, Pennsylvania. Yellow hued. Grainy nose. Refreshing malt palate lightly balanced with hops.

★ ★ ★
BEAMISH IRISH CREAM STOUT (Ireland)
Produced in Cork. Opaque, reddish brown hue. Sizable dense chocolaty cream head. Roasted palate, nose and flavor are less intense and body is not as full as its Irish stout competitors. Bittersweet finish.

★ ★ ★
BEAVER EXPORT LAGER BEER (England)
An international-style pale lager from Warrington. Golden liquid emanates a honeysucklelike floral nose. Malty hop palate with a touch of sweetness. Metallic hop nuances in finish.

★ ★ ★
BECK'S DARK BEER (West Germany)
Bremen-brewed beer with reddish brown hue and rocky, creamy tan head. Rich, semisweet malty nose and palate. Hops become most obvious in the finish, which is prolonged and slightly metallic. Medium-full bodied.

★ ★ ★ ★
BECK'S LIGHT BEER (West Germany)
Not a low-calorie light beer but a Bremener-Hamburger style pale lager crafted in Bremen. Refreshing carbonation. Vivid yellow coloring. Crisp nose and palate with a clean, hoppy finish.

★ ★ ★
BEER HAUSEN (Philippines)
Golden-hued international-style pale lager. Aromatic nose. Rounded body and fizzy mouthfeel.

★ ★ ★ ★
BELHAVEN SCOTTISH ALE (Scotland)
Created in Dunbar, this reddish, tea brown Scotch ale has a rocky beige head and a roasted malt nose and flavor. Medium full-bodied with a pleasant bitter finish. Thick lace.

★ ★
BELLE-VUE KRIEK LAMBIC (Belgium)
Opaque, cherry red hue. Cherry-tinged cream head. Bold cherry nose and flavor but brew is thinner and has less character than the better Kriek beers.

★
BERGHEIM BEER (United States)
A regional brew from Schmidt's of Philadelphia and Cleveland.

★ ★ ★
BERLINER KINDL WEISSE (West Germany)
A wheat beer. Pale golden hue that is characteristically hazy due to yeast. Intense citric nose. Sharp lemony flavor. Short-lived head. Traditionally laced with fruit (especially raspberry) syrup.

★ ★ ★ ★
BERNKASTELER PILS (West Germany)
Brewed since 1825 in Bernkasteler on the Mosel River. Golden hue. Rounded, semisweet malty nose and palate. Medium full-bodied. Hoppy midtaste and finish.

★ ★
BIECKERT (Argentina)
Brewed by Bieckert S.A. Off-white head. Yellow-gold liquid. Grainy nose. Develops harshness, beginning in midtaste.

★
BIG BARREL LAGER (Australia)
Short-lived, bleached-white head. Golden hue. Grainy nose. Gassy palate. Some harshness in finish.

★ ★ ★
BIG BEN ENGLISH BEER (England)
From Blackburn. This deep amber-bronze beer has a reserved, spicy, flowery nose and a bittersweet, somewhat chalky palate.

BIGFOOT ALE (United States)
See SIERRA NEVADA BIGFOOT ALE.

★
"BIG JUG" BEER (United States)
A budget-priced beer produced by Schoenling. Sold in half-gallon bottles.

★
BIG MAN MALT LIQUOR (United States)
Yellow-gold hue. Off-white head. Gassy mouthfeel. Heady finish with citric-sweet underpinning.

★ ★ ★ ★
BIOS COPPER ALE (Belgium)
Generous tan-cream head. Translucent strawberry-brownish-black brew. Rich, malty nose with bitter background note. Distinctive, fruit-tangy, semisweet flavor that lingers for seconds. Full-bodied and heady.

★ ★ ★
BISHOP'S ALE (England)
Brewed in Chelmsford, Essex. Also known as Ridley's Traditional Ale. Pale orange-amber. Large, light tan head. Hoppy flavor with sweetish backdrop. Detectable headiness.

★ ★ ★ ★
BITBURGER PILS (West Germany)
Crafted in Bitburg near the Luxembourg border. Golden hued. Malt-hop nose and palate with gliding hop conclusion.

★ ★ ★
BLACK FOREST LIGHT BEER (West Germany)
Produced by Dinkelacker in Stuttgart. This is not a low-calorie

light beer. Amber hued. Sweetish, caramelized malt nose with berrylike overtones. Bittersweet malt flavor.

★ ★
BLACK HORSE ALE (United States)
Brewed by Champale in Trenton, New Jersey. Pale honey-colored liquid that is clear, but not brilliant. Sweet-sour nose and palate.

★ ★ ★
BLACK HORSE PREMIUM ALE (United States)
Produced by the Fred Koch Brewery in Dunkirk, New York. Pale golden yellow. Malty, hoppy nose with hops preeminent in flavor and finish. This ale is not to be confused with the Black Horse Ale produced by Champale.

★
BLATZ BEER (United States)
A product of the G. Heileman Brewing Company.

☆
BLATZ LIGHT (United States)
A low-calorie light beer.

★
BLATZ LIGHT CREAM ALE (United States)
On the sweet side.

★ ★
BLITZ WEINHARD (United States)
American-style pale lager. Brewed in Portland, Oregon. Pale gold hue. Grainy malt nose; tart hop-malt palate.

★ ★
BLITZ WEINHARD BAVARIAN DARK BEER (United States)
Produced in Portland, Oregon. Opaque, ruby-brown hue. Sweet-ish profile lacks depth associated with top-notch dark beers.

★
BLUE FOX CREAM ALE (United States)
Brewed by the Simon Pure Brewery in Dunkirk, New York. Pale golden brew. Sweetish, grainy malt nose and palate. Bitter-harsh, chalky finish.

★ ★
BOHEMIA BEER (Mexico)
Golden hued. Sweetish nose. Gassy palate with a solventlike taste. Some hops in the finish.

BOMBARDIER ALE (England)
See CHARLES WELLS BOMBARDIER ALE.

★ ★
BOSCH BEER (United States)
Brewed in Wisconsin. Off-white head. Yellow hue. Grainy malt nose and palate. Crisp finish with tart-sharp note.

★ ★ ★ ★
BOULDER EXTRA PALE ALE (United States)
Crafted by Boulder Brewing Company. Creamy white head. Golden-orange color. Well-balanced, malt-dominated nose. Hoppy finish—again with balance. Sweet-sour notes in finish.

★ ★ ★ ★
BOULDER PORTER (United States)
Brewed in Boulder, Colorado. Chocolate-hued head. Opaque,

brownish black hue is ruby tinged. Scent is relatively dry considering its caramelized character. Chocolaty flavor. Finish has slight bitter and fizzy qualities yet is commendably smooth.

BRADOR MALT LIQUOR (Canada)
See MOLSON BRADOR MALT LIQUOR

BRAHMA BEER (Brazil)
An international-style pale lager brewed in Rio de Janeiro.

BRAND BEER
See HOLLAND BRAND BEER

BRASSEURS BIERE DE PARIS (France)
Formerly Lutèce. Pale tan head. Orange, copper-colored liquid. Heady, malty nose. Full, malty palate with a long hoppy finish.

★ ★ ★ ★
BRASSIN DE GARDE SAINT LEONARD (France)
Burgundy-style bottle sealed with a cork like that of a champagne bottle (though effervescence is only moderate). Yellowish tan head over orange-copper brew. Rich, sweetish roasted malt nose and palate with a balancing hop finish. Heady, winy character. Excellent with savory stews.

BRAUMEISTER PILSENER BEER (United States)
American-style pale lager brewed by Huber.

★ ★
BREAK (United States)
Produced by Christian Schmidt brewing company. Yellow color. Sweetish, grainy character. Slightly gassy palate.

★
BREUNIG'S BEER (United States)
American-style pale lager brewed by Walter Brewing in Eau Claire, Wisconsin.

★ ★
BREWER'S GOLD ALE (United States)
Firm hop character. Not as good as Ballantine India Pale Ale (q.v.).

★ ★ ★
BRIDGEPORT ALE (United States)
Produced by the Columbia River Brewing Company in Portland, Oregon. Ruby tinged. Caramelized nose and body with bittersweet chocolaty finish.

★ ★ ★
BRIDGEPORT GOLDEN ALE (United States)
Tannish cream head. Orangey-copper hue. Slightly sweet nose. Bitter almond finish with hop support. This and the Bridgeport Ale beers show promise, but need more depth and character to reach four-star status.

★
BRISA CERVEZA LIGERA (Mexico)
A low-calorie light beer that has more character than most low-calorie beers.

★ ★
BROKEN HILL LAGER BEER (Australia)
An international-style lager from Adelaide. Brassy gold tone. Slightly sweet nose. Light-medium body.

★
BROWN DERBY LAGER BEER (United States)
Made by General Brewing Company for Safeway Stores. On the thin and sweet side.

☆
BROWN DERBY LIGHT BEER (United States)
A low-calorie light beer.

★
BUB'S BEER (United States)
Produced by Walter Brewing of Eau Claire, Wisconsin.

★
BUCKHORN (United States)
An American-style pale lager.

★ ★
BUDWEISER (United States)
American-style pale lager brewed in many locations. Relatively large bead and bold carbonation. Bleached, short-lived head. Earthy, gassy and sweetish palate. Short finish.

BUDWEISER LIGHT (United States)
A low-calorie beer.

★ ★ ★ ★
BUFFALO BILL'S WHEAT BEER (United States)
Crafted by the minuscule Buffalo Bill's Brew Club in Hayward, California. Generous, creamy white head. Hazy (due to bottle conditioning) yellow-gold color. The typical wheat beer tartness is more obvious in this beer's scent than flavor. A refreshing brew, but the short-lived finish keeps it from earning a fifth star.

★
BULLDOG (Canada)
Sweetish, grainy nose and palate. Uneventful finish.

★ ★
BULL'S EYE DARK BEER (United States)
Brewed by the Simon Pure Brewery in Dunkirk, New York. Dark orange-brown liquid. Creamy tan head. Malty nose. Roasted malt palate and aftertaste.

★
BURGER BEER (United States)
A product of the Hudepohl Brewing Company, Cincinnati.

★ ★ ★
BURGERBRÄU (West Germany)
Vatted in Bamberg, northern Bavaria. Off-white head. Malt flavor with hint of tartness.

☆
BURGER LIGHT BEER (United States)
Produced by Hudepohl of Cincinnati. A low-calorie light beer.

★
BURGERMEISTER (United States)
"Burgie" is the nickname of this American-style pale lager from the West Coast.

★ ★
BURKE'S IRISH BRIGADE EXPORT STOUT (England)
Brewed in England, not in Ireland as name suggests. Opaque, ruby-brown hue. Chocolate cream-colored head. Intense, coarse roast malt nose. Astringent bitter palate and finish.

★
BUSCH (United States)
Produced by Anheuser-Busch, but not available in all states.

★ ★ ★ ★
CABLE CAR CLASSIC LAGER (United States)
Created in Berkeley, California. Golden liquid is hazy because beer is bottle conditioned. Sweetish malt nose and palate with suggestion of apricots. Finish has tart edge.

★
CANADA COUNTRY (Canada)
Golden pale lager. Grainy flavor. Exhibits some coarseness.

★
CANADIAN ACE PREMIUM (United States)
Not a "real draft beer" as the label promises, nor is it Canadian: it's produced by the Eastern Brewing Company in Hammonton, New Jersey.

★ ★ ★
CARDINAL SPECIAL BEER (Switzerland)
Pale creamy white head. Yellow brew. Moderate maltiness in nose and palate.

★ ★
CARLING BLACK LABEL CANADIAN STYLE (United States)
Another Heileman product. Golden in color with a simple, slightly sweet malt-hop flavor and an earthy backdrop.

CARLING BLACK LABEL LIGHT BEER (United States)
A low-calorie light beer from G. Heileman.

CARLING'S RED CAP CREAM ALE (United States)
Yellow-golden. Grainy nose and somewhat gassy palate.

★ ★ ★ ★
CARLSBERG BEER (Denmark)
International-style pale lager brewed in Copenhagen. Deep golden hue. Confident hoppy, malty nose. Hoppy palate and finish.

★ ★ ★
CARLSBERG ELEPHANT MALT LIQUOR (Denmark)
Amber-yellow. Malty nose. Slightly sweet, punchy and full-bodied, with a gassy bite. Strong metallic hop finish.

★ ★ ★
CARLSBERG SPECIAL DARK LAGER (Denmark)
Translucent liquid that is a dark tea brown color. Bittersweet roasted malt nose and palate with a bitter chocolate midtaste and aftertaste. Obvious alcohol. Medium full-bodied.

★ ★
CARTA BLANCA (Mexico)
Pale amber-colored brew with a sweet, flowery, grainy nose. Its sweetish, gassy palate contributes to its success in America.

★ ★
CARTA BLANCA DARK SPECIAL (Mexico)
Translucent coppery amber. Caramelized-sugar nose and palate. Somewhat gassy. Short finish for a dark beer.

★ ★
CASTLEMAINE XXXX EXPORT LAGER (Australia)
Produced in Brisbane. Pale golden brew with tart hops throughout.

★ ★ ★ ★
CELEBRATOR DOPPELBOCK (West Germany)
Opaque, rosy red brew crowned with tan head. Pronounced malty, somewhat caramelized nose. Sweetish malty palate. Full-bodied and potent. A brew with character.

★ ★ ★
CERES LAGER (Denmark)
Produced in Aarhus. Pale gold liquid. Moderately crisp taste. Celerylike flavor nuance.

★ ★
CHAMPION (United States)
Brewed by the Simon Pure Brewery in Dunkirk, New York. Deep orange-brown hue. Semi-thick creamy tan head. Sweet malty nose. Roasted malt finish.

★ ★ ★
CHARLES WELLS BOMBARDIER ALE (England)
Produced in Bedford. Clear, but not brilliant, coppery liquid. Large head. Rich, sweetish palate with flashes of saltiness and oiliness. Bitterness from roasted malt and hops.

★ ★ ★ ★
CHESBAY DOMESTIC LAGER (United States)
Brewed by Chesapeake Bay Brewing Company in Virginia. Dense, cream-tan head. Orange-copper color. Rich malty nose with earthy scent. Palate has chocolaty note. Has slightly more character than its sister brew (see below).

★ ★ ★ ★
CHESBAY GOLD DOMESTIC LAGER (United States)
Creamy head. Golden hued. Malty, chewy palate. This beer and its sister beer (see above) deserve four stars only when you can find a fresh sample. Unfortunately, Chesbay beers don't seem to travel or store well.

★ ★ ★
CHESHIRE ENGLISH PUB BEER (England)
Brewed by Greenall Whitley in Cheshire. Clover honey colored. Clear but not brilliant. Sweet, fruity, malty nose and palate with a hint of yeast. Slightly gassy mouthfeel.

★ ★ ★ ★
CHESTER GOLDEN ALE (England)
Vatted in Cheshire. Orange-tinted amber hue. Earthy, hoppy nose. Rounded foretaste gives way to slight bite.

★ ★ ★
CHIC BEER (France)
Brewed in Schiltigheim, Alsace. Golden hued. Bright white head. Hops more evident than the malt. Shy finish except for tangy notes.

★
CHIC LITE (France)
Thirty-nine calories per 8-ounce bottle equates to 59 for standard bottle. Golden color. Bleached white head. Citric nose with candied fruit echoes. Thin body and flavor. Brief aftertaste.

★
CHIHUAHUA (Mexico)
Relatively bland pale lager from the border town of Juarez. Pale golden tone. Fleeting head.

★ ★ ★ ★
CHIMAY ALE (Belgium)
Bottle-conditioned brew made by Trappist monks. Opaque, reddish brown hue. Dense head. Raspberry scent. Smooth palate except for some chalkiness. Sweetish backdrop.

★ ★ ★ ★
CHIMAY ALE GRANDE RESERVE (Belgium)
Opaque, ruby red-brown hue. Bottle conditioned. Fruity, vinous nose and palate with Madeira-like overtones. Fizzy mouthfeel.

★
CHINA BEER (Taiwan)
Produced in Taipei. Golden liquid. Bland nose. Ditto for flavor profile except for sweet-sour finale.

★
CHIPPEWA PRIDE LIGHT BEER (United States)
Produced by Jacob Leinenkugel Brewing Company in Wisconsin. White head. Pale gold liquid. Grainy malt nose and palate. Thin finish.

★ ★ ★
CHRISTIAN MOERLEIN (United States)
Crafted by the Hudepohl Brewing Company in Cincinnati. Amber golden liquid is topped by a creamy tan head. Fruity, malty nose with a somewhat gassy, malty palate. Firm hop finish.

★ ★
CHRISTIAN SCHMIDT CLASSIC (United States)
Brewed by Schmidt's of Philadelphia. Pale golden brew. Fresh, fruity, malty nose and palate with a sweet and hoppy background note.

★ ★ ★
CHRISTIAN SCHMIDT SELECT (United States)

An American-style pale lager. Golden hued. Malty nose with a touch of earthiness. Balanced malt-hop palate. More flavorful than the Christian Schmidt Classic.

★ ★
CINCI CREAM LAGER BEER (Canada)

A product of Carling O'Keefe Breweries. Pale gold. Grainy malt nose. Hop bite with some underlying sweetness in the palate.

★
CLUB CERVEZA PREMIUM BEER (Ecuador)

Brewed in Guayaquil near the equator.

★ ★ ★
COLD SPRING BEER (United States)

From Cold Spring, Minnesota. Gold colored. Earthy, fruity malt nose. Malty palate with a slight sharp afterbite.

★ ★ ★
COLD SPRING EXPORT (United States)

Pale golden. Earthy, fruity nose. Slightly sweet fruity palate with a faint medicinal aftertaste.

★ ★ ★ ★
COLLIN COUNTY BLACK GOLD BEER (United States)

Made by Reinheitsgebot Brewing Company in Plano, Texas. Tannish cream head. Opaque, ruby hue. Rich, sweet-accented caramelized nose. Full bodied with chocolaty-flavor note. Long finish. Slightly better than its sister brew, Pure Gold (see below).

★ ★ ★ ★
COLLIN COUNTY PURE GOLD BEER (United States)
Creamy white head. Yellow-gold hue. Nose has tropical fruit background note. Bitter-sharp hoppy flavor is this brew's signature.

★ ★
COLOMBIAN GOLD (Colombia)
This Colombian Gold is imported legally. Brewed in Bogotá. Grainy nose and palate with sweet accents.

★ ★
COLT 45 MALT LIQUOR (United States)
A product of the Heileman Brewing Company. Pale yellow hue. Sweetish, heady nose and palate without much complexity.

★ ★ ★ ★
COOPER (THOMAS & SONS) LAGER (Australia)
Brewed in Leabrook. Amber hued. Rich, fruity, malty nose. Hoppy taste with a distinctively caramelized, but not overly sweet, barley palate. Of the three fine Coopers rated four stars, this is a shade superior.

★ ★ ★ ★
COOPER (THOMAS & SONS) REAL ALE (Australia)
Light amber liquid that is not brilliant because it is bottle conditioned. Sweetish, cidery nose with an applelike, malty palate balanced by hops.

★ ★ ★ ★
COOPER (THOMAS & SONS) STOUT (Australia)
A bottle-conditioned brew. Dense, dark tan head over brownish black, opaque liquid. Tangy, roasted malt nose. Bittersweet malt palate with chocolaty undertone. Medium full-bodied. Obvious alcoholic strength.

★ ★
COORS BEER (United States)
From Golden, Colorado. Pale yellow hue. Pale nose, palate and aftertaste with a slight sweet and gassy infrastructure.

COORS LIGHT (United States)
A low-calorie brew.

★
COQUI 900 MALT LIQUOR (United States)
A product of Schmidt's of Philadelphia.

★ ★
CORONA (Puerto Rico)
Brewed in Santurce. Bleached white head on top of a golden-hued brew. Grainy scent. Slightly sweet taste.

★
CORONA EXTRA (Mexico)
Made in Mexico City. Pale golden color. Slightly gassy palate. Finish has sweet undertones.

★
COUNTRY CLUB MALT LIQUOR (United States)
A product of Pearl Brewing in San Antonio.

★ ★
CRISTAL (Portugal)
Pale gold hue. Sweetness is more evident in palate than nose.

★ ★ ★
CROWN LAGER BEER (Korea)
Produced in Seoul. Pale gold color. Slightly more character than Korean sister brew, OB Beer (q.v.).

★ ★ ★ ★
CUPIDO (Belgium)
Brewed in Buggenhout. Copper-amber liquid topped with pale cream-colored head. Caramelized malt flavor with hint of oats and overripe apricots in the background.

★ ★
CUZCO (Peru)
Golden-hued pale lager. Evidence of tanginess in scent and flavor.

★ ★ ★ ★
DAB BEER (West Germany)
Brewed by the Dortmunder Actien-Brauerei (DAB) in Dortmund. Its golden hue is a bit pale for a Dortmunder-style brew. Malty nose with a refreshing, balanced malt-hop flavor.

★ ★ ★ ★
DAB ORIGINAL SPECIAL RESERVE BEER (West Germany)
Golden hued with a malty nose. Crisp, firm metalliclike hop flavor and aftertaste.

★ ★
DAMM ALE (Spain)
Pale gold brew. Grainy nose. Sweetness overshadows other flavor attributes.

★ ★ ★
DANISH GOLD (Denmark)
Made in Randers. Brass-tinged gold hue. Trace of sweetness. Low-profile mineral-like mouthfeel.

★ ★ ★ ★
DE KONINCK (Belgium)
Created in Antwerp. Deep copper-amber hue. Pale cream-tan head. Sweetish, toasty malt nose. Bitter hop finale with smoky backdrop.

★ ★ ★
DEMPSEYS BEER (Ireland)
Dublin—brewed beer. Orange-amber hue. Rocky head. Hops dominate nose. Palate has peat, smoke character.

★ ★ ★ ★
DIEKIRCH LUXEMBOURG BEER (Luxembourg)
Golden hue with dense head. Fruity nose. Strong hop palate with a mouth-coating quality. Medium full-bodied.

★ ★ ★ ★
DIEKIRCH MALT LIQUOR (Luxembourg)
Light amber with a creamy head. Rich malty nose. Smooth, complex flavor with pronounced headiness and a hoppy finish.

★ ★ ★ ★
DINKELACKER BOCK BEER (West Germany)
Brewed in Stuttgart. Pale orange-amber. Zesty, spicy nose. Fruity, malty palate that sails on through to the finish. Medium full-bodied.

★ ★ ★ ★
DINKELACKER CD-PILS (West Germany)
Deep yellow hue. Tangy palate. Slighly bitter hoppy finish.

★ ★ ★
DINKELACKER DARK BEER (West Germany)
Displays a creamy tan head over opaque, reddish brown liquid. Sharp, sweet, malty nose. Full-bodied with a burnt maltose flavor that smacks of root beer. Cloying finish.

★ ★ ★ ★
DINKELACKER WEIZENKRONE (West Germany)
A wheat beer. Burnished golden hue. Characteristic haziness due to yeast. Substantial, long-lived head. Fresh, lemony, yeasty nose. Round, refreshing flavor. Many fans spike it with a slice of lemon or raspberry syrup.

★ ★
DIXIE BEER (United States)
Produced by Dixie Brewing Company of New Orleans. Pale gold colored. Fruity, malt nose and palate that finishes with faint hops.

DIXIE LIGHT (United States)
A low-calorie light beer.

★ ★ ★
DOMFÜRSTEN BIER (West Germany)
Pale gold hue. Relatively tame for a Bavarian-brewed beer.

★ ★ ★ ★ ★
DORTMUNDER-ACTIEN ALT (West Germany)
Reddish brown liquid that develops an enviable head. Rich, complex hop and malt aroma and flavor with a cedarlike touch.

★ ★ ★ ★
DORTMUNDER KRONEN CLASSIC (West Germany)
Brassy gold hue. Spicy accent to the floral, hop and malt aroma and flavor.

★ ★ ★ ★
DORTMUNDER UNION BEER (West Germany)
Considering this is a Dortmunder-style brew, the hue is unusually light. Floral esters spring forth in the aroma and hops in the malt-dominated flavor.

★ ★ ★
DORTMUNDER UNION DARK BEER (West Germany)
Deep amber color. Pale tan-cream-colored head. Would rate four stars if it were more complex.

★ ★ ★ ★
DORTMUNDER WESTFALIA BEER (West Germany)
Another fine product from the brewing city of Dortmund. Bronze-gold color. Fruity (somewhat figlike), malty nose and palate with a hop finish.

★ ★ ★ ★
DOS EQUIS (XX) BEER (Mexico)
Brewed in various locations throughout Mexico. Translucent amber-copper color. Sweetish roasted malt nose. Rich malt palate with a slight hop bite.

★ ★
DOS EQUIS (XX) SPECIAL LAGER (Mexico)
Pale golden. Fruity nose. Slightly hoppy palate and a bit gassy. Don't confuse this product with the better Dos Equis (XX) Beer.

DOUBLE DRAGON ALE (Wales)
See FELINFOEL DOUBLE DRAGON ALE.

DOUBLE MAXIM BROWN ALE (England)
See VAUX DOUBLE MAXIM BROWN ALE.

★ ★
DRAGON STOUT (Jamaica)
Prodouced in Kingston. Creamy chocolate brown head and dark reddish brown brew. Malty, heady nose and palate. Would receive three stars were it not for its unrefined bittersweet finish.

★ ★
DREHER BIRRA (Italy)
Amber-gold beer. Sweetish, mellow nose and palate. Could use more character.

★ ★ ★
DRESSLER BEER (West Germany)
Brewed in Bremen. Golden color. Crisp palate. Metalliclike hop aftertaste.

★
DREWRYS BEER (United States)
A Midwestern American-style pale lager from the Heileman group.

★ ★
DUBUQUE STAR BEER (United States)
The standard bearer of the Dubuque Star brewery (formerly Pickett Brewing Company). Pale yellow-gold. Sweetish malt-hop nose and aroma.

★ ★
DUKE ALE (United States)
Made by C. Schmidt & Son. Pale golden. Earthy and somewhat fruity, grainy malt nose. Malty palate finishes with tangy hops.

★
DUKE BEER (United States)
Gassier and thinner than Duke Ale.

★ ★ ★
DUNKEL WEIZEN BEER (United States)
Produced by Hibernia Brewing in Eau Claire, Wisconsin. Dense creamy tan head. Ruby-orange hue. Smoky malt nose and palate with sweet accents.

★ ★ ★ ★
DUVEL ALE (Belgium)
Crafted in Breendonk. Yellow-gold brew with a Gargantuan head. Fruity, tangy hops dominate the malt throughout, particularly in the aftertaste. Heady.

★
EAGLE LAGER BEER (India)
International-style pale lager from the makers of Golden Eagle (q.v.). Brewed in the state of Maharashtra in western India.

★
EAGLE PILSNER (United States)
Produced by Stevens Point Brewery in Steven Point, Wisconsin. Off-white head. Pale yellow-gold hue. Grainy malt nose and palate with sweetish underpinning.

★ ★
EAU CLAIRE ALL MALT LAGER BEER (United States)
Made by Hibernia Brewing in Wisconsin. Off-white head. Golden hued. Malty scent and palate have sweetish backdrop with hints of sourness. Fizzy mouthfeel.

★
E & B BEER (United States)
An American-style pale lager produced by the Iowa-based Dubuque Star brewery.

★
EDELWEISS LIGHT BEER (United States)
Has more flavor than the typical American-style low-calorie beer.

EDINBURGH ALE (Scotland)
See McEWAN'S EDINBURGH ALE

★ ★ ★ ★
EGGER BEER PILS (Austria)
From Unterradlberg. Golden liquid. Spicy, clovelike, malty nose and palate with a hoppy finish.

★ ★ ★ ★
EINBECKER UR-BOCK (West Germany)

Crafted in Einbeck, northern Germany. Full malty flavor and body with sweetish backdrop and conspicuous alcoholic content.

★ ★ ★ ★
EKU BAVARIA DARK RESERVE (West Germany)

From Kulmbach, Bavaria about 150 miles north of Munich. Large tan head tops opaque, ruby-brown liquid. Delicate roasted malt nose and bittersweet palate. Medium full-bodied. Semi-heady finish.

★ ★ ★ ★
EKU BAVARIA SPECIAL RESERVE (West Germany)

Brewed in Kulmbach. Yellow-gold hue. Malt undertone with a zingy mouthfeel.

★ ★ ★ ★
EKU EDELBOCK (West Germany)

Deep-toned golden hue. Sweetish malt nose. Vaguely reminiscent of the celebrated Trockenbeerenauslese German wines in terms of mouthfeel texture.

★ ★ ★ ★
EKU EXPORT (West Germany)

Made in Kulmbach. Pale golden brew. Toasty malt nose and palate. Moderate gassy bite. Finish is relatively quiet for an EKU product.

★ ★ ★
EKU HEFE-WEIZEN (West Germany)

Bavarian-style wheat beer bottled with live yeast. Golden hue. Expansive off-white head. Has a slightly more pronounced yeasty flavor than the plain EKU Weizen brew.

★ ★ ★ ★
EKU JUBILÄUMSBIER (West Germany)
Jubilee beer. Pale gold color. Off-white head. Malty palate with obvious alcohol. Stylish, extended finish.

★ ★ ★ ★
EKU KULMINATOR URTYP HELL 28 MALT LIQUOR (West Germany)
Deep coppery brew that emanates a rich, fruity, roasted malt nose. Sweet, moderately bitter palate with exceptionally heady midtaste and finish. One of the world's most potent brews—you can almost substitute it for gas in your Volkswagen.

★ ★ ★
EKU OKTOBERFEST (West Germany)
An Oktoberfest beer brewed in Kulmbach. Golden hue. Malty structure. Sweetish statement in aftertaste.

★ ★ ★
EKU PILS (West Germany)
Brewed in Kulmbach, Bavaria. Decent beer, but EKU has finer products. Yellow golden. Heady, hoppy palate. Tinny finish.

★ ★ ★
EKU WEIZEN (West Germany)
Bavarian-style wheat beer. Gold liquid with generous head. Sweet-tartness in nose and especially in palate. Fizzy.

ELEPHANT MALT LIQUOR (Denmark)
See CARLSBERG ELEPHANT MALT LIQUOR.

ERIE LIGHT LAGER (United States)
A low-calorie light beer from C. Schmidt.

★ ★ ★
ERLANGER (United States)
An amber, 100% barley malt beer made by Schlitz. Both bouquet and palate have roasted barley malt overtones with a hoppy backup. Relatively mild aftertaste.

★ ★ ★
ERZQUELL EDELBRÄU (West Germany)
A half-and-half blend of light and dark beers. Amber-brown hue. Sweetish, roasted-malt nose and palate with root beer-like accent.

★
ESQUIRE PREMIUM BEER (United States)
American-style pale lager from the Jones brewery in Smithton, Pennsylvania.

★
ESSLINGER (United States)
Produced in Wilkes-Barre, Pennsylvania by The Lion Inc.

★ ★ ★ ★
EULER LANDPILS (West Germany)
A product of the Euler Brewery in Wetzlar. Pale amber color. Fragrant malty nose. Rich, well-hopped palate.

★
FALLS CITY BEER (United States)
American-style pale-lager that is part of the Heileman empire.

★
FALSTAFF BEER (United States)
An American-style pale lager. This brew, the standard-bearer of the Falstaff conglomerate, is blander than it used to be.

FALSTAFF LITE BEER (United States)
A low-calorie light beer.

FARSONS SHANDY (Malta)
Brewed in Malta. Pale yellow-gold tone. Citric scent and flavor smacks of 7-UP. Shandy fans would be better off mixing an authentic shandy (part ale, part ginger beer).

★ ★ ★
FELINFOEL BITTER ALE (Wales)
Brewed in Llanelli on the Bristol Channel in Wales. Deep gold color. Less bitter and more sweet than name promises.

★ ★ ★
FELINFOEL CREAM STOUT (Wales)
Opaque, reddish brown. Dense, chocolate cream-colored head. Body lacks fullness of first-rate stouts.

★ ★ ★
FELINFOEL DOUBLE DRAGON ALE (Wales)
Produced in Llanelli. Creamy head. Relatively quiet flavor profile for an amber ale. Hops noticeable in finish.

★ ★ ★
FELINFOEL HERITAGE ALE (Wales)
Orange-amber ale made in southern Wales. Tannish cream head. Sweetish roasted malt nose and palate. Somewhat cloying.

★ ★ ★
FELINFOEL JOHN BROWN ALE (Wales)
Semiopaque, reddish brown brew. Rocky, cream-colored head. Aroma and flavor less intense than typical British brown ales.

★ ★ ★
FELINFOEL ST. DAVID'S PORTER (Wales)
Opaque, garnet-brown hue. Dense, chocolate cream-colored head. Fruity, cherrylike nose and palate. Slightly weak finish.

★ ★ ★
FISCHER MARCH BEER (France)
An Alsatian-style March beer (gentler than the Munich style). Brewed in Schiltigheim, near Strasbourg. Amber hued. Malty nose with suggestion of strawberry preserves. Palate a bit syrupy sweet.

★
FITGER'S BEER (United States)
American-style pale lager made in Minnesota by the August Schell Brewing Company.

★ ★
FIX (Greece)
Pale amber-gold. Sharpness in nose and palate that is typical of Greek beers.

★
FORT PITT (United States)
American-style pale lager made in the Jones brewery in Smithton, Pennsylvania.

★ ★
FOSTER'S LAGER (Australia)
From Melbourne. Brassy yellow. Sweetish, grainy nose and palate with some gassiness.

★ ★
FOX DE LUXE BEER (United States)
Made in Cold Spring, Minnesota. Gold colored. Citric nose. Tart, malty hop palate.

★
FOX HEAD "400" BEER (United States)
From Eastern Brewing of Hammonton, New Jersey.

★ ★
FRANKENMUTH BAVARIAN BEER (United States)
From Geyer Brothers of Frankenmuth, Michigan. Pale honey golden. Berrylike, yeasty nose. Tart and faintly sweet malty hop midtaste and finish.

★ ★
FRANKENMUTH BAVARIAN DARK BEER (United States)
Translucent, orange-brown color. Sweet, roasted-malt nose with a cloyingly bittersweet, chocolaty palate. Mouth-coating chalkiness.

★ ★ ★
FRANZIKUS HELLER BOCK (West Germany)
Made by Spaten in Munich. Golden color. Syrupy sweet malty character conspicuously evident from foretaste to finish. Full-bodied. Heady.

★ ★ ★
FRYDENLUND (Norway)
Pale yellow-gold brew produced in Oslo. Sweetish underpinning, especially in finish.

★ ★ ★
FULLER'S LONDON PRIDE (England)
English ale. Honeyed amber color with a dense, cream-colored head. Fruity, roasted-malt nose. Hoppy palate and finish.

★ ★ ★ ★
FÜRSTENBERG BEER (West Germany)
From the Black Forest town of Donaueschingen. Golden yellow hue. Clean malty aroma. Smooth texture and aftertaste.

GABLINGER'S EXTRA LIGHT BEER (United States)
A low-calorie light beer that predates Miller's Lite.

★
GENESEE BEER (United States)
From Rochester, New York.

★ ★
GENESEE CREAM ALE (United States)
Its hue is golden, its nose mild and its flavor sweetish mellow.

GENESEE LIGHT BEER (United States)
A low-calorie light beer.

★ ★
GENESEE 12 HORSE ALE (United States)
Golden hued. Moderate level of hops in aroma, flavor and aftertaste.

★ ★ ★ ★
GEORGE KILLIAN'S IRISH RED ALE (United States)
Brewed in Colorado by Coors using a proprietary Irish recipe. Reddish amber hue. Fruity, nutty, haunting malt aroma and flavor.

★ ★
GEYER'S LAGER BEER (United States)
Produced in Frankenmuth, Michigan. Golden hued. Nutty, malty nose and palate with balancing hops in midtaste and finish.

★
GIBBONS (United States)
American-style pale lager from Wilkes-Barre, Pennsylvania.

★
GILLEY'S BEER (United States)
From Shiner, Texas. Hoppier than Shiner Premium which is also brewed by the Spoetzl Brewery.

★ ★ ★
GIRAF MALT LIQUOR (Denmark)
Produced by Albani Breweries of Odense. Amber hued. Sweetish malt nose and palate with clean hoppiness. Pronounced heady midtaste and finish.

★ ★ ★
GLARNER BEER (Switzerland)
Brewed in Glarus in the Deutsch-Schweitz region. Yellow-tinted gold color. Hops slightly outplay the malt flavor.

★ ★
GOEBEL NATURALLY LIGHT GOLDEN LAGER (United States)
An American-style pale lager (not a low-calorie light beer) produced by The Stroh Brewery Company. Grainy, sweetish, malty nose and palate with hoppy counterpointing.

GOLD BEER (United States)
A low-calorie light beer formerly brewed by Olympia, now by Pabst.

GOLDEN BEAR (United States)
See THOUSAND OAKS GOLDEN BEAR.

★
GOLDEN CREST ALE (United States)
Brewed by the Simon Pure Brewery in Dunkirk, New York. Pale golden yellow tone. Off-white head. Slightly sweet, grainy nose with earthy note. Harsh, bitter-chalky finish.

★ ★
GOLDEN EAGLE LAGER BEER (India)
International-style pale lager. Deep golden hue. Background scent and flavor of rosewater with a metallic aftertaste. Low carbonation.

GOLDEN GATE MALT LIQUOR (United States)
See THOUSAND OAKS GOLDEN GATE MALT LIQUOR.

★ ★ ★
GOLD FASSL EXPORT BEER (Austria)
Vienna brewed. Off-white head. Deep yellow liquid. Sweet background note in both nose and palate. Medium-bodied.

★ ★ ★
GOLD FASSL PILS (Austria)
From the Viennese Ottakringer brewery. Golden hued. Faintly sweet, malty palate.

★ ★ ★
GOLD FASSL VIENNA LAGER (Austria)
A Viennese-made beer. Pale gold-yellow. Clean, modest malt flavor.

★ ★ ★ ★
GÖSSER EXPORT BEER (Austria)
From the Austrian state of Styria. This bright, golden liquid emanates a fruity, malty aroma. Crisp hoppy palate and lasting hop finish.

★ ★ ★ ★
GÖSSER STIFTSBRÄU (Austria)
Dark tan head over an opaque, burgundy-black-colored brew. Rich, sweet roasted malt nose and palate.

★ ★ ★ ★
GOUDEN CAROLUS (Belgium)
A dessert brew made in Mechelen. "Golden Carolus" is an opaque, ruby-brown brew. Small head. A rich, sweet, prune nose and palate. Potent.

★ ★
GRAIN BELT BEER (United States)
American-style pale lager marketed in the Midwest by G. Heileman Brewing Company. Crisp and clean. Simple but refreshing.

★ ★ ★ ★
GRANT'S ALE (United States)
Crafted by Yakima Brewing and Malting Company. Copper-orange hue. Haziness due to bottle fermentation. Fresh, rich, malty nose with obvious class and character. Pleasant bitter-hop finish.

★ ★ ★ ★
GRANT'S IMPERIAL STOUT (United States)
Brewed in Washington state. Chocolaty head. Black, opaque color. Bittersweet, chocolaty scent and flavor. Lingering bitter-hop finish.

GREAT WALL BEER (China)
Made in Tientsin, People's Republic of China.

★ ★ ★
GREENE KING ST. EDMUND SPECIAL PALE ALE (England)
Made in Bury St. Edmund, Suffolk, in Eastern England. Orange-

tinted amber hue. Nectarous background sweetness not fully integrated with overall flavor profile. Hop bite.

★ ★ ★ ★
GREENE KING SUFFOLK DARK ENGLISH ALE (England)
Semiopaque reddish brown color. Dense, cream-tan head. Roasted malt evident in bouquet and flavor. Trace of bitterness and powdery mouthfeel in aftertaste.

★ ★ ★ ★
GREENE KING SUFFOLK DARK ENGLISH ALE (England)
Semiopaque reddish brown color. Dense, cream-tan head. Roasted malt evident in bouquet and flavor. Trace of bitterness and powdery mouthfeel in aftertaste.

★ ★ ★
GRENZQUELL (West Germany)
Produced in Hamburg. Pale golden. Crisp palate. Hops overshadow malt flavor.

★ ★
GRIZZLY BEAR (Canada)
International-style pale lager. Copper-tinged, golden brew. Malt-grain flavor.

★ ★ ★ ★
GROLSCH LAGER BEER (Holland)
International-style pale lager. Deep gold colored. Fragrant malty nose with smooth, hop-dominated flavor and rich mouthfeel.

★ ★ ★ ★ ★
GUINNESS EXTRA STOUT (Ireland)
The godfather of stouts. Large, creamy, deep tan head with splendid lacework. Opaque, brownish black hue. Malty nose. Bitterness derives from scorched barley. (Note: The prodouct brewed

for consumption in Ireland has a creamier texture, a somewhat less hoppy and gaseous palate, and a less bitter aftertaste than the one exported to America. Though both rate five stars, the brewed-for-Ireland Guinness Stout has the edge in quality.)

★ ★ ★ ★
GULPENER HOLLAND PILSENER BEER (Holland)
Deep honey-gold. Off-white head. Tangy-crisp malt nose and palate.

★ ★ ★ ★
HACKER-PSCHORR BRÄUMEISTER PILS (West Germany)
Brewed in Munich. Golden tone. Fruity malt nose and palate. Hops expressed in aftertaste.

★ ★ ★ ★
HACKER-PSCHORR FEST BEER (West Germany)
Golden hue. Body is a shade thinner than typical Munich-brewed Fest beers. Moderate bitter hop finish.

★ ★ ★ ★
HACKER-PSCHORR MÜNCHEN DARK BEER (West Germany)
Deep orange-amber color. Tannish cream head. Roasted malt aroma and flavor. Drier than most Munich dark beers.

★ ★ ★ ★
HACKER-PSCHORR MÜNCHEN EDELHELL EXPORT (West Germany)
Munich *helles* with a pale golden hue. Floral scent. Semisweet malty background note. Mild hops.

★ ★ ★ ★
HACKER-PSCHORR MÜNCHEN LIGHT BEER (West Germany)
Not a low-calorie light beer but a Munich *helles*. Pale golden color. Floral, estery odor. Malty flavor with hoppy background and fresh finish.

★ ★ ★ ★
HACKER-PSCHORR MÜNCHEN WEISS BEER (West Germany)

Wheat beer brewed in Munich. Pale amber hue. Characteristic haziness due to yeast. Yeasty, grapefruity nose and palate. Müncheners customarily flavor it with a lemon slice or a dash of fruit syrup.

★ ★ ★ ★ ★
HACKER-PSCHORR ORIGINAL OKTOBERFEST BIER (West Germany)

This deep amber beer is topped by a dense, pale beige head. Clean malty nose. Rich, bittersweet, roasted malt flavor is apparent in foretaste and midtaste. Mellows to a fine malty aftertaste. Full-bodied. High alcohol.

★ ★
HAFFENREFFER PRIVATE STOCK MALT LIQUOR (United States)

Yellow gold hue. Earthy, grainy malt nose. Palate is slightly heady and tart.

★ ★
HAMM'S (United States)

"Born in the land of sky blue waters," says the motto. Pale yellow color. Innocent nose and palate.

HAMM'S SPECIAL LIGHT (United States)

A low-calorie brew.

★ ★ ★
HANSA BEER (Norway)

Produced in the town of Bergen. Brassy amber colored. Fruity, malty nose and palate. Tangy, hoppy finish.

★ ★ ★
HARBOE BEAR BEER (Denmark)
Pale gold liquid. Moderately crisp, in the Danish style. Malt-hop aftertaste.

★ ★ ★
HARP LAGER BEER (Ireland)
International-style pale lager from Dublin. Pale golden yellow. Rich, sweet, fruity esters in nose. Slightly sweet, malty, hoppy palate that fades quickly.

★ ★
HEIDELBERG BEER (United States)
American-style pale lager from the Heileman brewing empire.

★ ★
HEILEMAN'S OLD STYLE (United States)
American-style pale lager. Pale golden yellow. Slightly sweet and grainy. Malt and hops in equilibrium.

HEILEMAN'S OLD STYLE LIGHT (United States)
A low-calorie light beer.

★ ★
HEILEMAN'S SPECIAL EXPORT BEER (United States)
Pale gold hue. Noticeably crisper and hoppier than the typical Heileman brands.

★
HEILEMAN'S SPECIAL EXPORT LIGHT (United States)
A low-calorie (155 per bottle) beer. Sweet note from start to finish.

★ ★ ★ ★
HEINEKEN LAGER BEER (Holland)
From Amsterdam. Golden yellow liquid. Rich, fruity, malt nose and palate; well balanced. Hoppy finish.

★ ★ ★
HEINEKEN SPECIAL DARK BEER (Holland)
A dark reddish brown brew. Roasted malt nose and palate with a sweet, bitter backdrop.

★ ★ ★ ★
HENNINGER BIER (West Germany)
From Frankfurt. Golden-hued brew emanates a fruity, hoppy-malt nose. Palate has roasted malt touch with hops toward the end.

★ ★ ★
HENNINGER DARK BIER (West Germany)
Translucent, deep rosy brown liquid. Roasted malt nose and palate with a tart ending.

★ ★ ★ ★
HENNINGER DOPPELBOCK (West Germany)
Dense tan head over an opaque, rosy brown brew. Subtle, bittersweet malt nose. Sweet, roasted malt palate with background bitterness. Heady finish. Medium full-bodied.

★ ★ ★
HENRY WEINHARD'S PRIVATE RESERVE BEER (United States)
Brewed in Portland, Oregon. A premium beer with a golden hue. Floral, citric hops obvious in the nose. Malty palate dips in the midtaste. Hop finish.

★ ★ ★ ★
HERFORDER PILSNER (West Germany)
Made in Herford. Deep amber hue. Fruity nose with a hop-dominated malt palate and finish.

★ ★
HERITAGE ENGLISH ALE (England)
Produced in Sunderland. Orange-copper hue. Cloying, caramelized malt palate.

★ ★ ★
HERMAN JOSEPH'S 1868 (United States)
Produced by Coors in Colorado. Full gold hue. Malty nose and palate. Hops and roasted malt in finish.

★
HERRENBRÄU LIGHT (West Germany)
Brewed in Bayreuth. Relatively thin nose, flavor and body for a Bavarian beer. Curious watermelonlike background note.

★ ★ ★
HERRENBRÄU PILSENER (West Germany)
Golden hue. Citric-tart nose. Sweet-sour malty palate.

★ ★
HERRENBRÄU WEIZEN (West Germany)
Wheat beer with sweet-tart, Madeira-like nose and palate. Lingering tart finish.

★ ★ ★ ★
HERRENHÄUSER LAGER BEER (West Germany)
Brewed in Hanover. Liquid is golden yellow; head is generous. Laid-back aroma gives little hint of the forthcoming crisp hop flavor and finish.

★ ★ ★
HET KAPITTEL WATOU PRIOR (Belgium)
An ale. Opaque, ruby-brown color. Sweet, fruity nose with yeasty, coffee undertones. Sweet, fizzy palate.

★ ★
HIBERNIA BOCK BEER (United States)
Produced by Hibernia Brewing in Eau Claire, Wisconsin. Tan head. Ruby-copper hue. Sweet, malty nose and palate have boderline cloying quality.

★ ★
HINANO (Tahiti)
International-style pale lager fashioned in Papeete. Pale gold. The "Girl" (that's what *hinano* means) is fruitier, fuller-bodied and more refreshing than typical tropical brews.

★ ★ ★ ★
HOEGAARDEN WHITE BEER (Belgium)
Wheat brew made in Hoegaarden. Pale gold hue. Sizable head. Yeasty, floral malt-wheat nose. Yeast-sharp palate with slightly puckerish finish.

★ ★ ★
HOFBRÄU BAVARIA DARK RESERVE (West Germany)
Brewed in Kulmbach, Bavaria, this dense, reddish brown beer sports a pale nutty-colored head. Malty nose. Slight tingle and feel of alcohol on palate. Full bodied. Medicinal finish.

★ ★ ★ ★
HOFBRÄU BAVARIA LIGHT RESERVE (West Germany)
Not a low-calorie light beer. Brewed in Kulmbach, Bavaria (not Munich as "Hofbräu" might suggest). Clear, but not brilliant. Honey golden hue. Spicy malt superstructure with hoppy finale.

★ ★ ★ ★
HOFBRÄU BAVARIA OKTOBERFEST BEER (West Germany)

From the famous Hofbräuhaus in Munich. Deep amber. Clean, sweet malt nose. Background bitterness from roasted malt and, to a lesser degree, hops. Potent and full-bodied.

★ ★ ★ ★
HOFMARK WURZIG HERB PILSENER (West Germany)

Pilsner beer brewed in Cham, 20 miles from Czechoslovakia. Yellow gold. Sweetish malt nose and palate with background dry, bitter-hop accent. Slightly sharper than sister brew, Hofmark Wurzig Mild Export (see below).

★ ★ ★ ★
HOFMARK WURZIG MILD EXPORT (West Germany)

Produced in eastern Bavaria. Yellow-gold hue. Scent and flavor have sweet-sour malty notes. Noticeable dry, hop finish with sharp underpinning.

★ ★ ★
HOLLAND BRAND BEER (Holland)

Produced in Wylre in a brewery that dates from 1340. Yellow golden. Somewhat sweetish malt-hop bouquet. Slight gassy bite. Sold in gimmicky white-painted bottle. Also marketed as "Brand" and "Royal Brand."

★ ★ ★ ★
HOLSTEN LAGER BEER (West Germany)

A Bremener-Hamburger style beer. Golden yellow hue, ample head and commanding nose.

★
HOMBRE (Mexico)

The "Man" from Juarez, Chihuahua is not a macho brew—flavor is weak. Grainy palate with sour hint.

★ ★ ★ ★
HOPFENPERLE (Switzerland)
Golden hued. Rich mouthfeel with hoppy finish and fancy lace.

★ ★
HUBER (United States)
The standard bearer of Huber Brewing in Wisconsin. Golden hued. Slightly tart nose. Smooth, gentle malt palate with a hoppy aftertaste.

★
HUDEPOHL BEER (United States)
Produced by the Hudepohl Brewing Company in Cincinnati, Ohio.

★ ★ ★
HUDEPOHL BOCK (United States)
Deep reddish copper with a creamy tan head. Malt nose. Roasted malt palate with a slightly sweet, mouth-coating quality. Medium full-bodied.

★ ★
HUDEPOHL OKTOBERFEST (United States)
Coppery amber. Roasted malt nose with earthy touch. Bittersweet, slightly coarse, roasted malt flavor and finish.

HUDY DELIGHT BEER (United States)
A low-calorie beer produced by Hudepohl.

★ ★ ★ ★
HÜRLIMANN STERN BRÄU (Switzerland)
Crafted in Zurich. Pale golden liquid. Fruity, pearlike aroma. Sweetish but crisp hop-malt flavor.

★
HUSSONG'S CERVEZA CLARA (Mexico)
Bland lager with few distinguishing characteristics except for its sweet undertones.

★ ★
I-C GOLDEN LAGER (USA)
Krausening method used by its maker, the Pittsburgh Brewing Company. White head. Golden body. Grainy nose and flavor. Background sweetness swells in aftertaste.

★
I.C. LIGHT (United States)
A low-calorie light beer produced by the Pittsburgh Brewing Company.

★ ★ ★
INNSBRUCK LAGER BEER (Austria)
Produced in Innsbruck. Pale gold brew. Mild hop, slightly sweet finish.

IRISH BRIGADE EXPORT STOUT (England)
See BURKE'S IRISH BRIGADE EXPORT STOUT.

★ ★
IRON CITY BEER (United States)
A premium-priced product of the Pittsburgh Brewing Company. Pale gold. Grainy malt nose. Clean, but relatively mild palate.

★ ★ ★
IRON HORSE MALT LIQUOR (Canada)
Brewed in Prince George, British Columbia. Golden color. Malt-hop midtaste followed by hoppy, somewhat sweet finish.

★ ★ ★
ISENBECK EXPORT DELUXE (West Germany)
Brewed in Hamm. Deep gold hue. Fruity, malty nose and palate with a hop finish.

★
JACOB BEST PREMIUM LIGHT BEER (United States)
Produced by Pabst. Jacob Best is maltier and better than the typical American-style light beer.

★ ★ ★
JACOBINS GUEUZE LAMBIC (Belgium)
Deep tea brown-amber hue. Sweetish, sherry-like nose. Fruity, cidery palate with a slight puckerish finish.

★ ★ ★
JACOBINS KRIEK LAMBIC (Belgium)
Semiopaque cherry red-brown color. Cherry-tinged white head. Both nose and palate have intense tart-cherry attributes reminiscent of Jell-O.

★ ★
JÄGERWAHL DAS BOCKBIER (United States)
Made in New Orleans by Dixie Brewing. Reddish brown brew with a bittersweet, malt flavor. Concludes with lingering smoke and chalky mouthfeel.

★
JAX BEER (United States)
This "New Orleans tradition" is now made in San Antonio, Texas by the Pearl Brewing Company.

★ ★ ★ ★
JEVER PILSENER (West Germany)
Brewed in Jever near the North Sea. Cream-white head. Yellow hued. Malty nose. Malt-hop palate. Hoppy finish with toasted nut accent.

JOHN BROWN ALE (Wales)
See FELINFOEL JOHN BROWN ALE.

★ ★ ★ ★
JOHN COURAGE EXPORT BEER (England)
Produced in London. Translucent amber-orange liquid. Slightly sweet, partially roasted malt nose and palate with hops in the finish.

★ ★ ★
JOHN PEEL EXPORT BEER (England)
Made in Blackburn, in the Midlands. Creamy tan head. Copper-gold liquid. Subdued yeast scent. The hop-dominated flavor helps shield the brew's somewhat cloying sweetish flavor profile.

★
JOLIE BLONDE (United States)
Produced for Bayou Brew Brothers in New Iberia, Louisiana by Pearl Brewing Company, San Antonio, Texas. Pale yellow hue. Sweetish grainy nose and palate. Slight harshness in finish.

★
J.R. EWING'S PRIVATE STOCK (United States)
A product of Pearl Brewing in San Antonio, Texas.

★
JUL BREW LAGER (Gambia)
West African beer produced in Banjul. Pale golden. Grainy nose and palate. Short-lived head.

★ ★ ★ ★
JULIUS ECHTER HEFE-WEISSBIER (West Germany)
Yellow-gold wheat beer. Obvious yeast in aroma and flavor. Gently puckering palate and finish.

★
KAIER'S SPECIAL BEER (United States)
An American-style pale lager produced by the Christian Schmidt brewery.

★ ★ ★
KAISERBRÄU BAMBERG BEER (West Germany)
Golden hued. Malt nose and palate with toasty background note.

★ ★ ★ ★
KAISERDOM PILSENER (West Germany)
Brewed in the northern Bavarian city of Bamberg. Pale gold color. Tart malt palate with slightly hop-bitter finish.

★ ★ ★
KAISERDOM RAUCHBIER (West Germany)
Smoked Bavarian beer from Bamberg. Opaque, dark brown color. Creamy tan head. Roasted barley malt nose. Smoky flavor becomes especially pronounced in the aftertaste.

★ ★ ★
KALBACK LAGER (Sweden)
A product of the Pripps brewery in Gothenburg. Amber liquid. Flowery nose. Edgy hop-malt palate with a lingering hop finish. Calorie count is only 110—less than a Michelob Light (q.v.)

★
KANGAROO BEER (Australia)
International-style pale lager vatted in Mildura. Golden tone. Nose and flavor lack desirable intensity.

★ ★ ★ ★
KAPUZINER WEIZEN (West Germany)
Yellow-gold hue. Large, dense, cream-colored head. Expansive fruit-floral nose with sweet-sour malt tones. Smooth palate for a wheat beer. Sprightly mouthfeel. Low-keyed bitter puckering aftertaste.

★ ★
KARLOVACKO LIGHT BEER (Yugoslavia)
Not a low-calorie light beer. Honey golden. Applelike nose and palate that carry through to the finish. Some hops.

★
KASSEL BEER (United States)
Produced by Pearl Brewing Company of San Antonio, Texas.

★
KB LAGER (Australia)
International-style pale lager brewed in Sydney. Golden hued. Thin palate.

★ ★
KEGLE BRAU (United States)
Produced by Cold Spring Brewing of Minnesota. Generous apple-scented nose emanates from the gold-colored brew. Mellow mid-taste. Hoppy finish.

★
KELLERBRAU LAGER (England)
From Bedford. Pale amber colored. Grapefruit-orange peel nose. Tart palate.

KILLIAN'S IRISH RED ALE (United States)
See GEORGE KILLIAN'S IRISH RED ALE.

KINDL WEISSE (West Germany)
See BERLINER KINDL WEISSE.

★
KING COBRA MALT LIQUOR (United States)
An Anheuser-Busch product. Pale yellow. Heady. Cloyingly sweet, somewhat gassy profile.

★
KINGFISHER LAGER BEER (India)
A golden-hued brew made in the state of Kerala in southern India. Celery seed nose. Oily finish.

★ ★ ★
KINROSS SCOTCH ALE (England)
Made in England despite "Scotch" name. Deep ruby-orange-amber hue. Creamy head. Detectable roast malt scent, cherry-tart flavor notes and powdery tooth-coating mouthfeel.

★ ★ ★ ★
KIRIN BEER (Japan)
The best of the imported Japanese beers. Golden hued. Fruity, aromatic nose and subdued palate make this beer ideal with light-flavored foods such as Japanese tempura.

★ ★ ★
KIRIN BOTTLE DRAFT BEER (Japan)
Brewed in Tokyo. Not as crisp or flavorful as regular Kirin.

KIRIN LIGHT BEER (Japan)
Brewed in Tokyo. Better than most low-calorie light beers but still rates zero stars.

★ ★ ★
KLOSTER PILSENER (West Germany)

Produced in Hamm, Westphalia. Gold tone. Malt and hop interplay in midtaste and finish.

★ ★ ★ ★ ★
KLOSTER SCHWARZBIER (West Germany)

Previously marketed as Kulmbacher Monkshof Dark Beer. Brewed by Mönchshof Bräu in Kulmbach, Bavaria. The liquid is opaque and reddish brown with a milky tan head. Rich, malty nose and flavor. Comparatively dry for a Bavarian dark beer. Full-bodied.

★ ★
KNICKERBOCKER NATURAL BEER (United States)

A product of Christian Schmidt. Pale golden. Earthy, sweetish malt and grainy nose. Ditto for the palate but add a bit of hops. Steely aftertaste.

★ ★ ★ ★
KOCH'S GOLDEN ANNIVERSARY BEER (United States)

Created by the Fred Koch Brewery of Dunkirk, New York. Straw-gold colored. Expansive malty nose with a hop thrust. Rich hoppy palate that is well balanced with malt. Gentle hop finish.

★ ★ ★
KOEHLER (United States)

A golden-hued beer from Schmidt's. Slightly sweet, malty nose. Palate exhibits interesting play between malt and hops.

★ ★ ★
KOFF FINNISH BEER (Finland)

Created in Helsinki. Golden hued. Earthy aroma. Somewhat hollow midtaste. Hoppy finish.

★ ★ ★ ★
KOFF IMPERIAL STOUT (Finland)

Dense, deep camel-tan head. Brownish black, totally opaque hue. Rich, bittersweet malt nose with a touch of chocolate. Complex burned-malt taste with a bitter chocolate note. Full-bodied.

★ ★ ★ ★
KÖNIG-PILSENER (West Germany)

Cream-colored head over a deep golden lager. Fresh, malty nose. Hops balance the malt in the palate. Steely hop finish.

KONINCK (Belgium)

See DE KONINCK.

★ ★ ★
KRAKUS LIGHT BEER (Poland)

Not a low-calorie brew. Produced in Zywiec, this pale gold beer has a citrus-apple nose, and a sweet, cidery, slightly smoky flavor.

★ ★ ★ ★
KRONEN CLASSIC ALT DARK (West Germany)

An ale brewed in Dortmund. Orange-amber hue. Tannish cream head. Profile starts with sweetish malt flavor and ends with a bitter-hop, somewhat chalky finish.

★ ★ ★ ★
KRONENBOURG (France)

From Alsace. Golden-hued beer with a fruity, malty nose. Elegant, balanced malt-hop flavor that is well suited to classic French and other delicate cuisines.

★ ★ ★
KRONENBOURG DARK (France)
Dark reddish brown with a spicy, fruity (tangerinelike) nose. Sweet-better palate. Refreshing. Medium full-bodied.

★ ★ ★ ★
KROPF EDEL PILS (West Germany)
Crafted in Kassel in central Germany. Golden-yellow color. Ripe peachy nose. Smooth, malty midtaste but a slight bite evolves in the finish.

★
KRUEGER BEER (United States)
Part of the Falstaff conglomerate. American-style pale lager. Noted for being the first beer packaged in a can.

★ ★ ★
KULMBACHER HELLER MAIBOCK (West Germany)
Golden-hued brew made by Erste Kulmbacher Actienbrauerei. Toasty malt nose with sweetish accent. Fruity palate is even sweeter.

★ ★ ★ ★
KULMBACHER MÖNCHSHOF OKTOBERBIER (West Germany)
This pale, honey-amber beer is produced in Kulmbach, Bavaria. Sweetish malty nose and palate. Creamy texture. Full-bodied. High alcohol.

★ ★ ★ ★
KULMBACHER MONKSHOF AMBER LIGHT BEER (West Germany)
Not a low-calorie light beer. Golden in color. Malty aroma edged with honey. Detectable roasted malt flavor.

★ ★ ★ ★
KULMBACHER MONKSHOF KLOSTER-BOCK (West Germany)
Deep reddish amber with a pale beige head. Sweet roasted malt nose and flavor. Creamy texture. Medium full-bodied.

★ ★ ★
KULMBACHER REICHELBRÄU (West Germany)
Deep golden yellow hue. Fruity, malt nose. Flavor lacks depth and complexity typical of top-rated brews vatted in Kulmbach, Bavaria.

★ ★ ★ ★
KULMBACHER SCHWEIZERHOF-BRAU BOCK (West Germany)
Brewed in Bavaria. Large, creamy head. Unlike most bock beers available in the United States, this one has a yellow-gold as opposed to a dark hue. Malty nose and palate with sweet note.

★ ★ ★ ★
KÜPPERS KÖLSCH (West Germany)
World's best-selling Kölsch, an ale from the Bonn and Cologne area. Pale, brassy gold color. Refreshingly crisp palate with lactic acid accent.

★ ★ ★ ★
KWAK (Belgium)
Made in Buggenhout near Brussels. Opaque, garnet-brown brew with creamy tan head. Heady scent and flavor with anise accent. Dry mouthfeel aftertaste.

☆
LA (United States)
Has 50% less alcohol than regular beer. It also has 50% less flavor and body.

★ ★
LABATT'S "BLUE" BEER (Canada)
Produced in many plant locations throughout Canada. Thin, sweetish grainy nose and palate with a bite. Woody, alelike after-taste.

★ ★
LABATT'S 50 CANADIAN ALE (Canada)
Yellow golden. Sweetish grainy nose and palate with some hops. A slightly cloying aftertaste.

LABATT LIGHT (Canada)
A low-calorie light beer.

★ ★ ★ ★
LA BELLE STRASBOURGEOISE (France)
Brewed by Fischer of Alsace. Coppery bronze liquid topped by a beige head. Distinctive, fruity, berrylike aroma with a bready note. Smoky, tart palate.

★ ★ ★ ★
LEEUW (Holland)
Vatted in Valkenburg. Brass-tinged, pale gold color. Pleasing, balanced hop flavor. Nutty hint in aftertaste.

★ ★ ★ ★
LEFFE BLONDE ALE (Belgium)
An abbey ale that has a honey-gold hue, a sweetish apricot malt-hop nose and a heady palate.

★ ★ ★ ★
LEFFE DARK ALE (Belgium)
Opaque, reddish-black color. Soft, roasted malt nose. Bittersweet malt flavor that crescendoes in midtaste and finish. Has sufficient balancing hops. Heady.

★ ★ ★ ★
LEFFE RADIEUSE ALE (Belgium)

A translucent, orange-red abbey ale. Sweetish malt-hop aroma. Fruity bittersweetness that is strong in the midtaste and even more so in the aftertaste. Smooth for its type. Heady.

★ ★
LEINENKUGEL'S BEER (United States)

Made by the Jacob Leinenkugel Brewing Company of Chippewa Falls, Wisconsin. Golden hued with an earthy nose. Malty palate that has some background tartness and saltiness.

★ ★
LEINENKUGEL'S BOCK BEER (United States)

Orangy copper. Sweetish roasted malt nose that leads to a slightly sweeter, caramelized malt palate.

★
LEINENKUGEL'S LIGHT (United States)

"Lennie's Light" is a low-caloried brew.

★ ★
LEOPARD DELUXE LAGER BEER (New Zealand)

Produced by the Leopard Brewery in Hastings. Golden hued. Sweetish grainy nose with a tart background. Ditto for the palate.

★ ★
LEOPOLD PILS (Belgium)

Label boldly displays three stars, but this brew from Leuven deserves only two. Grainy, slightly tart nose with a touch of harshness in finish.

★ ★ ★ ★
LIBERTY ALE (United States)

Brewed by Anchor Brewing Company of San Francisco,

California. Honey hued. Generous, creamy head. Fruity, hop nose. Hints of mandarin orange in scent and palate. Malty infrastructure.

★
LIEBOTSCHANER SPECIAL CREAM ALE (United States)
Produced by The Lion, Inc. in Wilkes-Barre, Pennsylvania.

LIGHT SCHLITZ (United States)
A low-calorie light beer brewed in various regional locations.

★ ★ ★
LINDEMANS FARO LAMBIC (Belgium)
Produced in Vlezenbeck. Orange-amber coloration. Dense, cream-tan head. Intensely fruit-sweet nose and palate with winy undertones. Astringent, tart finish.

★ ★
LINDEMANS FRAMBOISE LAMBIC (Belgium)
A raspberry lambic beer brewed in Vlezenbeck. Opaque, cherry red hue. Raspberry-tinged, cream-colored head. Lambics can be sweet, but this brew goes a bit too far. Its sweetness is redolent of Jell-O and berry soda pop. Tart, puckery finish.

★ ★ ★
LINDEMANS GUEUZE LAMBIC (Belgium)
Produced at the Lindeman brewery in Vlezenbeek. One of the most champagnelike of beers. Active carbonation produces an expansive head over the deep amber-colored liquid. Sour fruit nose. Tart, salty palate with slightly astringent aftertaste.

★ ★ ★
LINDEMANS KRIEK CHERRY BEER (Belgium)
A lambic beer. Strawberry cream head over deep, strawberry

syrup-colored liquid. Sour fruit nose. Decidedly sweet-sharp, cherry-flavored palate with prolonged astringency.

★ ★
LION LAGER BEER (South Africa)
Pale orangy amber-hued brew. Fruity, tangerinelike nose and palate.

★
LIONSHEAD PILSNER BEER (United States)
Brewed by Lion in Wilkes-Barre, Pennsylvania. White head. Pale yellow color. Sweet scent and flavor dominate an otherwise tame beer.

LITE BEER (United States)
From the Miller Brewing Company. A low-calorie light beer. Ever so slightly better than most light beers but it is still a zero-star brew.

★
LITTLE KINGS CREAM ALE (United States)
A regional favorite from the Schoenling Brewing Company, Cincinnati.

★ ★ ★
LOHRER BIER (West Germany)
Produced in Lohr, Bavaria. Honey-gold color. Sweetish malt nose and palate with a smooth hop finish.

LONDON LIGHT LAGER BEER (England)
A London-brewed low-calorie (96 per bottle) beer.

★ ★ ★
LONDON PRIDE (England)
Tannish head tops a tea-hued liquid. Sweetish hop midtaste and finish.

★ ★
LONE STAR BEER (United States)
From San Antonio, Texas. Pale golden. Fruity, slightly sweet aroma. Gassy palate with smoky background.

LONE STAR LIGHT (United States)
A low-calorie light beer.

★ ★ ★
LORD CHESTERFIELD ALE (United States)
Produced in Pottsville, Pennsylvania by Yuengling, America's oldest extant brewery. Pale golden hue. Fragrant, faintly sweet nose with a hoppy fillip. Slightly gassy palate.

★ ★ ★ ★
LORIMER'S TRADITIONAL SCOTCH ALE (Scotland)
Brewed in Edinburgh. Amber tea color. Creamy beige head. Caramelized malt aroma with rich sweet flavor. Full-bodied.

★ ★ ★
LÖWENBRÄU (United States)
Brewed by the Miller Brewing Company. Pale golden hue. Grainy malt aroma and flavor, a bit on the sweet side. Firmer structure than Miller High Life. (Note: Three major brewing companies [in Germany, the U.S. and Switzerland] make a line of Löwenbräu products. The Miller-brewed line is inferior to the other two. The one made in Munich, West Germany is the best but, unfortunately may not be imported into the United States because Miller bought the exclusive American marketing rights from the Munich firm. Miller did not buy the rights from the Swiss Löwenbräu firm, and hence, that Swiss line is still being marketed here.)

★ ★
LÖWENBRÄU DARK SPECIAL (United States)
A coppery brown beer from Miller Brewing Company. Sugary sweet nose and palate that lacks the body and complexity of both the Swiss and German dark Löwenbräus.

★ ★ ★ ★
LÖWENBRÄU ZURICH (Switzerland)
Yellow golden. Fruity, flowery nose. Smooth, rich, mouth-coating quality.

★ ★ ★
LÖWENBRÄU ZURICH EXPORT DARK (Switzerland)
Dark coppery brown with an earthy nose. Sweet, fruity, roasted malt palate.

★
LÖWENBRÄU ZURICH LIGHT (Switzerland)
Low-calorie (95 per bottle) beer made in Zurich. Maltiness is more pronounced than in its American counterparts.

★ ★
LUCKY LAGER (United States)
American-style pale lager. Pale golden. Sweetish tart, hoppy nose and a grainy malt, somewhat gassy palate.

★ ★ ★ ★
MacANDREWS SCOTCH ALE (Scotland)
Creamy brown head on top of a bronze-hued brew. Rich, moderately sweet nose. Bittersweet caramel flavor lingers into the aftertaste.

★ ★ ★
MACCABEE (Israel)
Brewed in Netanya. Pale yellow-gold hue. Malt-grain nose and

palate with sweetish background note. Noticeable drop-off of flavor in finish.

★ ★ ★ ★
MACKESON TRIPLE STOUT (England)
A London-brewed Whitbread product. Brownish black, opaque liquid topped by an upsurging creamy brown head. Sweet roasted malt nose. Scorched-malt palate that is sweeter than that of Guinness. Lactic backdrop. Full-bodied.

★
MAGNUM MALT LIQUOR (United States)
A product of the Miller Brewing Company.

★ ★ ★
MAISEL BAYRISCH (West Germany)
Brewed in the Wagnerian city of Bayreuth. Gold hue. Sweetish malt scent. Slightly caramelized malt flavor. As with most Maisel-brewed beers shipped to America, this one is relatively thin bodied for a German product.

★ ★ ★ ★
MAISELBRÄU SPEZIAL (West Germany)
From Bayreuth. Golden amber color. Tannish cream head. Roasted-malt nose and palate with a chocolaty background note.

★ ★ ★
MAISEL EXPORT (West Germany)
Vatted in Bayreuth. Golden liquid. Off-white head. Malt-hop nose and palate.

★ ★ ★
MAISEL FEST-BIER (West Germany)
Pale amber color. Beverage is decent but its flavor, sweetness and

overall character lack complexity of the top-rated Munich-brewed Octoberfest beers.

★ ★ ★
MAISEL'S DAMPF BIER (West Germany)
Amber hued. Tannish cream head. Dampf means "steam" in German. Decent, but hardly holds a candle next to California's Anchor Steam Beer.

★ ★ ★
MAISEL'S DUNKEL (West Germany)
Opaque, ruby-brown. Creamy tan head. Tart-edged roast malt in midtaste and finish.

★ ★ ★
MAISEL'S HEFE WEISSBIER (West Germany)
Bavarian-style wheat beer bottled with live yeast. Amber hued. Sweet-tart nose and palate. Noticeable yeastiness, especially in the taste.

★ ★ ★
MAISEL'S ORIGINAL 1887 (West Germany)
Gold liquid. Shades of sweetness are evident from foretaste through aftertaste.

★ ★ ★
MAISEL'S PILSENER (West Germany)
Pale gold hue. Has sweet malt flavor characteristic of Bavarian brews, but is crispier and hoppier.

★ ★ ★ ★
MAISEL'S TRADITIONAL (West Germany)
Coppery amber color. Heady, malt nose. Roasted malt palate. Full-bodied.

★ ★ ★
MAISEL'S WEIZEN (West Germany)
Bavarian-style wheat beer. Pale gold hue. Tall head. Yeasty, sweet-tart scent and taste.

★ ★
MAISEL'S WEIZEN BOCK (West Germany)
Bavarian-style wheat beer. Deep orange-amber hue. Enormous, tannish cream head. Bananalike background scent and flavor. Sweetness is a bit cloying and finish has coarse touch.

★ ★
MANILA GOLD PALE PILSEN (Philippines)
Pale yellow-gold liquid topped with bleached white head. Grainy nose. Muted chlorinelike sensory impression in midtaste and finish.

★ ★ ★
MARKSMAN LAGER BEER (England)
Creamy-hued head. Yellow-gold liquid. Grainy malt nose and palate. Hop finish with slight puckery metallic undertone.

★
MASTER BREW (United States)
Brewed and distributed around Eau Claire, Wisconsin.

★ ★
MASTER'S III (United States)
Brewed by Coors in Golden, Colorado. A joint venture of Coors, Molson and Kaltenberg. Cream-white head. Golden hued. Off-dry scent and flavor. Crisp, sprightly finish.

★
MATT'S LIGHT PREMIUM BEER (United States)
A low-calorie light beer from West End Brewing of Utica, New

York. Relative to American light beer standards, this is above average.

★ ★
MATT'S PREMIUM BEER (United States)
Yellow golden liquid. Malty nose with traces of fruit and earthiness. Crisp palate.

MAXIMATOR (West Germany)
See AUGUSTINERBRAU MUNCHEN MAXIMATOR.

★ ★ ★ ★
MAXIMILIAN (West Germany)
Off-white head. Golden hued. Caramelized malt discernable in nose and palate. Noticeable headiness.

★ ★ ★
MAXIMUS SUPER (United States)
A product of West End Brewing in Utica, New York. Golden color. Malty, hoppy nose with an earthy backdrop. Heady, malty palate. Medium body.

★ ★ ★ ★
McEWAN'S EDINBURGH ALE (Scotland)
Dark tan head. Translucent copper-brown brew. Roasted malt nose. Bittersweet malty palate.

★ ★ ★ ★
McEWAN'S SCOTCH ALE (Scotland)
Brewed in Edinburgh. Tan head. Semiopaque brown liquid with a red winelike tinge. Sweet, roasted malt nose and flavor. Body is substantial. Aftertaste is invitingly bitter.

★ ★ ★ ★
McEWAN'S TARTAN ALE (Scotland)
Red-tinged brown color. Full, sweetish malty nose and palate. Bittersweet finish.

★
MEISTER BRAU (USA)
Made by the Miller Brewing Company. Bleached white head. Pale yellow body. Sweetish grainy nose and palate without much character.

★ ★
McSORLEY'S CREAM ALE (United States)
A product of C. Schmidt & Sons from Philadelphia. Pale amber. Green, citric nose. Well hopped but, unfortunately, it smacks of hop pellets. The old McSorley's was much better.

★ ★ ★
METEOR BIERE D'ALSACE (France)
Brewed in the Alsatian village of Hochfelden. Brass-tinged gold coloration. Hops predominate in aftertaste.

★ ★ ★
MICHELOB (United States)
Brewed in many locations throughout the country. Pale golden liquid with a loose-knit, moderate head. Sweetish rice and barley-malt nose and palate. Less gassy than typical American brews but more so than typical quality imports.

★ ★ ★
MICHELOB CLASSIC DARK (United States)
Opaque, ruby-tinged brown hue. Cream-colored head. Smoother taste than most mass-produced American dark beers. Slightly fizzy mouthfeel.

★ ★
MICHELOB LIGHT (United States)

From Anheuser-Busch. Not technically a low-calorie light beer because it has 134 calories (96 is typical) per 12-ounce bottle. Pale yellow hue with a sweetish nose and palate.

★
MICKEY'S MALT LIQUOR (United States)

Part of the Heileman empire. A high octane soda pop (sweet and gassy) brew.

★ ★
MILLER HIGH LIFE (United States)

Compared to Budweiser (q.v.). Miller has a less generous nose and a slightly sweeter, less gassy palate. It is also smoother and has a mouth-coating quality.

★ ★
MILLER HIGH LIFE BOTTLE DRAFT (United States)

Similar to the regular Miller High Life, but has a denser head and chewier texture.

★ ★
MILLSTREAM LAGER BEER (United States)

Brewed by Millstream Brewing Company in Amana, Iowa. Creamy tan head. Golden hued. Malty nose with sweet notes. Sweetness is also noticeable in foretaste, but becomes overwhelming in finish.

★
MILWAUKEE BRAND PREMIUM (United States)

A product of Eastern Brewing Company of Hammonton, New Jersey.

★
MILWAUKEE'S BEST (United States)
Thin-flavored beer brewed by the multi-brewery Gettleman enterprise.

★
MODELO ESPECIAL (Mexico)
Brewed in Modelo and not so "especial."

★ ★ ★
MOLSON ALE (Canada)
Yellow golden. Sweetish, fruity nose and palate with mild hops. More polished than its two closest competitors. Labbatt's 50 and O'Keefe Canadian ales (qq.v.).

★ ★
MOLSON BRADOR MALT LIQUOR (Canada)
Pale gold. Sweet-sour notes in scent and flavor. Heady.

★ ★ ★
MOLSON CANADIAN BEER (Canada)
Golden liquid. Tangy hop nose reminiscent of spruce and citrus. Hoppier than Molson Ale or Golden Ale. Sweetish background.

★ ★
MOLSON GOLDEN ALE (Canada)
Sweetish, mildly citric nose and palate.

MOLSON LIGHT (Canada)
A low-calorie (109 per bottle) beer.

★ ★ ★ ★
MÖNCHSHOF AMBER LIGHT BEER (West Germany)
Not a low-calorie beer. Brewed in Weissenbrunn, Bavaria.

Creamy tan head, golden amber hue. Sweet malty nose. Slightly biting flavor.

★ ★ ★ ★
MÖNCHSHOF FESTBIER (West Germany)
Copper-amber liquid. Cream-tan head. Roasted malt nose and palate. Good balance for potent brew. Slight astringency in finish.

MÖNCHSHOF OKTOBERBIER (West Germany)
See KULMBACHER MÖNCHSHOF OKTOBERBIER.

MONKSHOF AMBER LIGHT BEER (West Germany)
See KULMBACHER MONKSHOF AMBER LIGHT BEER.

MONKSHOF KLOSTER-BOCK (West Germany)
See KULMBACHER MONKSHOF KLOSTER-BOCK.

★
MONTE CARLO (Guatemala)
Pale lager. Curious grainy flavor dominates the sensory profile.

★
MON-LEI (People's Republic of China)
Snowy, fleeting head. Pale gold hue. Grainy, somewhat biting palate.

★
MOOSEHEAD CANADIAN LAGER BEER (Canada)
Produced in New Brunswick and Nova Scotia. A cult beer among some American collegians. Organoleptically, it has a sweet, lemon nose and palate with a soda pop personality.

★ ★ ★
MORETTI PILSNER (Italy)
An international-style pale lager brewed in Udine. Golden hued with a chalk white head. Full, flowery and hoppy nose. Tart foretaste with a hollow midtaste. Sweet, salty finish.

★ ★ ★
MORT SUBITE KRIEK (Belgium)
Brewed near Brussels. Opaque, cherry-red hue. Dense, sizable cherry-tinged cream head. Cherry attribute more pronounced in flavor than in aroma. Sprightly sweet-bitter puckery finish.

★
MOUNTAIN CREST (Canada)
Pale yellow liquid. Thin, sweetish palate.

★ ★
MÜNSTERHOF FRENCH BEER (France)
An Alsatian lager. Golden hue. Mild hop-malt flavor. Touch of astringency in finish.

★ ★ ★ ★
MURPHY EXPORT STOUT (Ireland)
Compared to Guinness Extra Stout (q.v.), Murphy has a smoother palate but is not as rich or full-bodied, and its head is a shade paler.

★
MURREE LAGER (Pakistan)
Brewed in Rawalpindi. Pale gold with a tart palate.

★
M.W. BRENNER'S AMBER LIGHT (United States)
This semi-low-calorie (118) brew almost earns two stars. Pale amber color. Hops in evidence from sniff to finish.

★ ★
NARRAGANSETT OLD STYLE PORTER (United States)
A product of Falstaff. Opaque, brownish black tinged with cherry red. Rich, sweetish, roasted-malt nose. Bittersweet flavor lacks needed complexity and finish.

★
NARRAGANSETT LAGER (United States)
Part of the Falstaff conglomerate. Used to be better in the old days.

★ ★
NATIONAL BOHEMIAN BEER (United States)
American-style pale lager from Heileman. Slightly sweet note throughout. Refreshing malt-hop balance.

★
NATIONAL PREMIUM PALE DRY BEER (United States)
A Heileman product brewed in Baltimore by Carling.

NATURAL LIGHT (United States)
A low-calorie light beer from Anheuser-Busch.

★ ★ ★
NEGRA MODELO DARK BEER (Mexico)
Deep amber beer. Creamy tan head. Caramel sweet flavor. Fair lace.

★
NEKTAR BEER (Yugoslavia)
Amber-gold brew. Loose knit head quickly dissipates. Quick finish.

★ ★
NEPTUN DANISH PILSENER (Denmark)
Pale yellow brew with off-white, cream-hued head. Slight hop astringency.

★ ★ ★ ★ ★
NEW AMSTERDAM AMBER BEER (United States)
Amber beer with a reddish tinge brewed in New York State in the English fashion. Invigorating Cascade and Hallertauer hop flavor and finish. Small head. Trace of sweetness. Smooth texture.

★ ★ ★ ★
NEWCASTLE BROWN ALE (England)
Brewed in Newcastle-upon-Tyne, Northumberland. Translucent, brownish red. Creamy beige head. Roasted malt nose with hoppy backdrop. Medium full-bodied. Bittersweet palate—the bitterness stays through to the finish.

★ ★ ★ ★
NEWCASTLE LIGHT ALE (England)
Vatted in Newcastle-upon-Tyne, in northern England. Rich malt-hop scent. Flavor profile starts sweetish ends tangy-dry.

★ ★ ★
NIKSICKO PIVO (Yugoslavia)
Brewed in Niksic. Amber colored. Watery nose hardly sets the stage for the full flavor of the roasted malt and hoppy palate. Slight bitter finish.

★
900 MALT LIQUOR (United States)
Manufactured by Pearl Brewing in San Antonio, Texas.

NOCHE BUENA (Mexico)
Christmas beer. Ruby, coppery brown hue. Semisweet, rich roasted barley nose, flavor and aftertaste.

NORDIK WÖLF LIGHT (Sweden)
Has slightly more calories than the average low-calorie light beer (110 vs. 96 per bottle) but it offers slightly more flavor.

NORTHERN CANADIAN LIGHT BEER (Canada)
A low-calorie light beer from Northern Breweries in Ontario.

NORTH STAR BEER (United States)
A product of Cold Spring Brewing of Minnesota. Golden liquid emanates a fruity nose. Moderate palate building to a hop aftertaste.

NUT BROWN ALE (England)
See SAMUEL SMITH'S NUT BROWN ALE.

OATMEAL STOUT (England)
See SAMUEL SMITH'S OATMEAL STOUT.

OB BEER (Korea)
An international-style pale lager made in Seoul. Pale yellow. Grainy nose and palate.

★ ★ ★
OBERDORFER WEISSE (West Germany)
Produced in Marktoberdorf, Bavaria. Pale gold hue. Sizeable head. Malt-wheat nose with spicy accent. Sweet-tart palate and finish.

★ ★
O'KEEFE CANADIAN ALE (Canada)
Produced by Carling O'Keefe in Toronto. Golden hued. Somewhat sweet, grainy nose and palate with a touch of hops. Curious chalky aftertaste.

★ ★ ★
OKOCIM FULL LIGHT (Poland)
From Warsaw. Not a low-calorie light beer. Pale golden hued. Obvious metallic mouthfeel in midtaste and finish.

OLD BOHEMIAN LIGHT BEER (United States)
Made by Eastern Brewing Corp of Hammonton, New Jersey.

★
"OLD DUTCH" BRAND (United States)
From the Pittsburgh Brewing Company.

★
OLDE ENGLISH "800" MALT LIQUOR (United States)
Brewed in various cities across the country.

★
OLDE FROTHINGSLOSH (United States)
A gimmick brew with a roly-poly bathing suit queen on the label. Not for sophisticated palates.

★ ★ ★ ★
OLD FOGHORN BARLEYWINE STYLE ALE (United States)

A product of Anchor Brewing Company of San Francisco. Orange-beige head over a dark orange-copper brew. Intense, sweet, roasted malt nose with obvious hops and alcohol. Bittersweet malty palate with convincing hops in midtaste and finish. Medium-full to full-bodied. Heady. For savoring, not guzzling.

★
OLDE PUB TAVERN BREW (United States)

A regional beer found around Philadelphia and Cleveland.

★ ★
OLD GERMAN BEER (United States)

Made in Pottsville, Pennsylvania by Yuengling. Pale yellow-gold. Fruity, earthy nose. Malty, hoppy palate.

★
OLD GERMAN PREMIUM LAGER (United States)

Produced by the Pittsburgh Brewing Company.

★
OLD KELLER (United States)

An American-style pale lager.

★
OLD MILWAUKEE (United States)

A product of the Joseph Schlitz Brewing Company.

OLD MILWAUKEE LIGHT (United States)

A low-calorie light beer brewed by Schlitz.

★ ★ ★ ★
OLD PECULIER ORIGINAL YORKSHIRE ALE (England)
Opaque, brown liquid topped by a dense, tan head. Pure malt nose. Rich, sweet malty palate. Creamy texture. Full-bodied.

★
OLD SHAY GOLDEN CREAM ALE (United States)
Made by the Fort Pitt Brewing Company in Smithton, Pennsylvania.

★
OLD TIMER'S LAGER (United States)
A product of the Walter Brewing Company of Eau Claire, Wisconsin.

★ ★
OLD VIENNA LAGER (Canada)
Produced in Toronto by Carling O'Keefe. Golden hued. Earthy, fruity nose and palate with a sweetish backdrop.

★ ★
OLYMPIA (United States)
Gold hue. Clean, mild malty nose and palate with a weak finish.

OPTIMATOR (West Germany)
See SPATEN DOPPELSPATEN OPTIMATOR.

★ ★ ★ ★
ORANJEBOOM (Holland)
Brewed in Rotterdam. Brass-gold hue. Pungent sharpness in nose and palate.

★
ORTLIEB'S (United States)
A product of Christian Schmidt Brewing Company in Philadelphia.

★ ★ ★ ★
ORVAL TRAPPIST ALE (Belgium)
A triple-fermented Trappist ale with lively effervescence. Creamy tan head. Pale amber-orange liquid. Distinctive spicy, guavalike and heady nose. Allspice palate with a slightly woody, bitter mouthfeel in the finish. Throws a sediment.

OUR SPECIAL ALE (United States)
See ANCHOR'S "OUR SPECIAL ALE."

★
PABST BLUE RIBBON (United States)
A shadow of its former self. Brewed in various locations.

PABST EXTRA LIGHT (United States)
A low-calorie light beer.

★ ★
PABST SPECIAL DARK BEER (United States)
Coppery hue. Mild and light-bodied for a dark brew. Sold on tap.

★
PACIFICO CLARA (Mexico)
Produced in Mazatlan. Grainy, cornlike palate with sweet accent. Low to medium bodied.

★ ★ ★
PAINE'S PALE ALE (England)
Large head caps butterscotch-hued liquid. Fruity malt nose with hints of dried apricots. Smoky palate.

★ ★ ★ ★
PALM ALE (Belgium)
Brewed in Londerzeel, near Brussels. Amber liquid topped with tannish cream head. Soft caramelized malt nose and palate with bitter-orange accent. Counterbalancing hops in finish.

★
PANACH' (France)
Made by the makers of "33" in Paris. Drinkers weaned on sugary soda pop should love this one.

★
PANAMA (Panama)
Pale gold color. Unappealing gassy-sweet palate.

★ ★ ★ ★
PATRIZIER PILS (West Germany)
Brewed in Nuremberg. Golden hued with a greenish coppery tinge. Cream-colored head. Smooth, gentle flavor with a sweet undertone. Mild, hoppy finish.

★ ★ ★ ★
PAULANER MAIBOCK (West Germany)
Paulaner's golden-hued "May Bock" is sweetish but less so than its Ur-Bock brew. Hops noticeable in finish. Full-bodied.

★ ★ ★ ★
PAULANER MÜNCHNER MÄRZEN (West Germany)
March beer brewed in Munich. Deep orange-amber coloration.

Dense, tannish cream head. Rich, sweetish malt scent. Pleasant roasted malt character from midtaste to finish.

★ ★ ★ ★
PAULANER OKTOBERFEST (West Germany)
Crafted in Munich. Golden brew topped by off-white head. Malty nose and palate with tart-sweet backdrop. Heady.

★ ★ ★ ★
PAULANER PILS (West Germany)
Produced in the world-famous brewing city of Munich. Pale gold color. Has sweetish backdrop. Raw malt flavor, especially in aftertaste.

★ ★ ★ ★
PAULANER SALVATOR (West Germany)
A Doppelbock from Munich. Deeply gold colored. Roasted malt nose. Bitter note emerges in palate. Heady.

★ ★ ★ ★
PAULANER ULTBANNERISCHES WEISSBIER (West Germany)
Wheat beer brewed in Munich. Gold hue. Expansive head. Tart-yeast nose and palate. Slightly sweeter than Paulaner's regular Weizen beer. Fizzy mouthfeel.

★ ★ ★ ★
PAULANER ULT-MÜNCHNER DUNKEL (West Germany)
Opaque, ruby-brown hue. Sweetish roasted malt nose and palate. Heady. Somewhat chalky mouthfeel.

★ ★ ★ ★
PAULANER UR-BOCK (West Germany)
This Paulaner "Old/Original Bock" is a light rather than dark-hued, Munich-style bock beer. Intense sweet-malt nose and palate. Heady and full-bodied.

★ ★ ★ ★
PAULANER URTYP 1634 (West Germany)
Golden hue. Fruity nose with a citric note. Malty palate. Hops are most obvious in finish.

★ ★ ★ ★
PAULANER WIES'N-MÄRZEN (West Germany)
An amalgamation of wheat and March brews. Copper-tinted amber. Fruity-tart nose. Soothing mouth-coating palate.

★ ★ ★ ★
PAULANER WEIZEN (West Germany)
Munich-brewed, Bavarian-style wheat beer. Pale gold hue. Large head. Sweet tart nose and palate with yeast accent.

★
PEARL (United States)
American-style pale lager produced in San Antonio, Texas.

PEARL LIGHT (United States)
A low-calorie light beer produced by the Pearl brewery.

★
PEKING BEER (People's Republic of China)
Gold color liquid. Miniscule head. Detectable sweet and sour fruity flavor in midtaste and finish.

★ ★ ★
PERONI PREMIUM BEER (Italy)
Brewed in Naples. Golden hued. Mild malty nose with a sharp, hoppy midtaste.

PFEIFFER (United States)
American-style pale lager that was formerly brewed in Detroit but is now made elsewhere by Heileman.

PICKETT'S PREMIUM (United States)
American-style pale lager. Pale gold hue. Faintly sweet malt-hop nose and palate.

PICKETT'S PREMIUM LIGHT (United States)
A low-calorie brew.

PICKWICK ALE (United States)
A golden-hued brew with a mild, malt-hop nose. Hops become most noticeable in midtaste and finish.

PIELS DRAFT STYLE PREMIUM (United States)
Not really a "draft" style because it is pasteurized.

PIELS LIGHT (United States)
The label proclaims that it is "A classic light beer brewed in the style of the renowned light beer of Pilsen, Czechoslovakia. Unique for its balance of exquisite lightness and delicious full flavor." What blatant hype!

PILGRIM'S PRIDE SPECIAL RESERVE (United States)
Brewed by the Simon Pure Brewery in Dunkirk, New York. Amber hued. Slightly musty nose. Sweetish palate.

★
PILSEN (Peru)
Brewed in Callao just north of Lima.

★
PILSENER CLUB (United States)
American-style pale lager produced by Pearl Brewing of Texas.

PILSENER OF EL SALVADOR (El Salvador)
Made in San Salvador City. Pale gold tone. Weak flavored except for a curious background note reminiscent of decaying oranges.

★ ★ ★ ★ ★
PILSNER URQUELL (Czechoslovakia)
Created in Plzeň. Amber golden. Rich, expansive, fruity nose with malt and hops in evidence. Complex palate: malt and hops counterpoint each other, producing a thrilling balance. Relatively full-bodied for a pale lager. Pleasant, dry, woody, hop finish.

★ ★ ★ ★
PINKUS ALT (West Germany)
Ale produced in the brewery of Pinkus Müller, a noted restaurant in Münster. Honey golden hue. Yeast contributes slight haze to its clarity. Pinkus Alt is acidic like a wheat beer and has a sweet echo. Locals add fruit syrup.

★ ★ ★
PINKUS PILS (West Germany)
Honey golden hue. Clear, but not brilliant. Noticeable hoppiness with some balancing maltiness. Citric undertones.

★ ★ ★ ★
PINKUS WEIZEN (West Germany)
A wheat beer made from approximately one-third wheat, two-

thirds barley malt. Acidic but this does not intimidate the palate. Some drinkers flavor it with lemon or a teaspoon or two of fruit syrup.

★
PIPING ROCK (United States)
Brewed by the Simon Pure Brewery in Dunkirk, New York. Pale golden hue. Earthy, slightly sweet nose. Grainy malt palate. Noticeable bitter-harsh finish.

★ ★
PLANK ROAD (United States)
Product of Miller Brewing Company. Yellow-gold hue. Off-white head. Slightly more body than Miller High Life.

★ ★ ★
PLOTZ-BRAU WEISSBIER (West Germany)
Wheat beer brewed in Peissenberg in Bavaria. Large head. Orange-tinted gold liquid. Tart nose and palate.

★
P.O.C. (United States)
An American-style pale lager also known as Pilsener On Call.

★ ★ ★
POINT BOCK BEER (United States)
From the Stevens Point Brewery of Wisconsin. Dark orange copper color. Deep malty nose. Rich, bittersweet roasted malt palate with playful hops in the aftertaste. Medium full-bodied.

★ ★ ★
POINT SPECIAL BEER (United States)
Straw-gold color. Rich, malty nose. Pleasant malt-hop balance in the flavor.

★ ★ ★ ★
POPE'S '1880' BEER (England)
Vatted in the English Channel city of Dorchester. Creamy tan, reasonably dense head. Orangy copper liquid. Well-hopped nose and palate. Bittersweet finish with a developing citric accent.

★ ★
PORETTI (Italy)
An international-style pale lager. Amber gold. Uncomplex nose and palate. Weak finish.

★ ★ ★ ★
PORTLAND TRADITIONAL LAGER (USA)
A Maine Coast Brewing product, but made in Eau Claire, Wisconsin. Dense, creamy tan head. Amber-hued liquid. Generous malty nose with gratifying hop accents. Lingering finish.

★ ★
PORT ROYAL EXPORT "PILSENER STYLE" (Honduras)
Golden hued. Slightly gassy. Aftertaste exhibits touch of astringency.

★
PRESIDENTE (Dominican Republic)
Pale gold hue. Earthy nose. Sweetish cornlike grainy palate with powdery mouthfeel in finish.

★ ★ ★ ★
PRIOR DOUBLE DARK BEER (United States)
A product of the Christian Schmidt Brewing Company. Tan head over opaque reddish brown liquid. Rich roasted malt nose. Mouthfilling, sweetish chocolate and roasted malt palate. Pleasant, lingering finish.

★ ★ ★
PUNTIGAM EXPORT (Austria)
From the city of Graz. Honey golden hue. Fruity, berrylike nose. Slightly tart malt palate with firm hops in the finish.

★ ★
RADEBERGER (East Germany)
International-style pale lager brewed in East Berlin. Golden hued. Relatively tame for a German beer.

★ ★ ★
RAFFO BIRRA (Italy)
Brewed in Rome by Peroni. Yellow golden. Flowery nose. Sweetish malty and sharp hoppy palate.

★ ★ ★
RAINIER ALE (United States)
Part of the Heileman Brewing Company empire. Brewed in Seattle, Washington. Coppery amber colored. Hoppy and somewhat heady.

★
RAINIER BEER (United States)
An American-style pale lager. Part of the Heileman brewing empire.

RAINIER LIGHT BEER (United States)
A low-calorie light beer.

RAUCHBIER (West Germany)
See KAISERDOM RAUCHBIER.

★ ★ ★ ★
RAUCHENFELS (West Germany)
Orangey copper color. Tannish cream head. *Rauch* means "smoke" in German. Stones heated in a beechwood fire are added to the brewing vessel, though the resulting smoky flavor is more reminiscent of hickory.

★ ★
READING LIGHT PREMIUM BEER (United States)
Not a low-calorie brew. Produced by Schmidt's. Pale gold with a grainy malt nose. Tangy malt palate with a quick finish.

★
RED BULL MALT LIQUOR (United States)
A Stroh-Schlitz product. Heady with unsophisticated sweetness, especially in finish.

★
RED STRIPE LAGER (Jamaica)
International-style pale lager. Thin flavor and body.

★
RED WHITE & BLUE (United States)
An American-style pale lager.

★
RESCHS PILSENER EXPORT (Australia)
Brewed by the makers of Tooth in various Australian locations.

★
RHEINGOLD (United States)
Has slipped in quality over the years.

RHEINGOLD EXTRA LIGHT BEER (United States)

A low-calorie light beer.

RHEINLANDER BEER (United States)

Brewed in Seattle by Rainier, a subsidiary of G. Heileman Brewing Company.

RHINELANDER EXPORT (United States)

Produced by Huber of Wisconsin. Golden hued with a hoppy and faintly earthy nose. Smooth, malty hop palate. Somewhat unctuous mouthfeel.

★ ★ ★

RINGNES DARK (Norway)

From Oslo. Dark reddish brown opaque liquid topped by a tan head. Earthy, sweet malt nose. Gassy and somewhat cloying palate. Medium to medium-full-bodied.

★ ★ ★

RINGNES IMPORTED SPECIAL (Norway)

Deep golden with a large off-white head. Flowery, roselike nose. Relatively mild palate for a northern European brew.

RINGNES LOW (Norway)

Low-calorie (90 per bottle) and low-alcohol beer made in Oslo.

★ ★ ★

RINGNES SPECIAL BOCK BEER (Norway)

Opaque, brownish black color. Sweet, roasted malt nose. Somewhat bittersweet, cloying molasseslike palate. Medium full-bodied.

★ ★ ★
RINGNES SPECIAL CHRISTMAS ALE (Norway)
Brassy amber-hued holiday brew from Oslo. Cream-colored head. Roasted malt aroma and flavor with sweetish tones. Finish has hint of cola drink sweetness.

★ ★ ★ ★
RITTER BRAU BOCK-MALT LIQUOR (West Germany)
Made in Dortmund. Golden hue. Rich malt nose and taste. Heady.

★ ★ ★
RITTER BRAU DARK BEER (West Germany)
Deep bronze color. Roasted malt nose and body with hops in support.

★ ★ ★ ★
RITTER BRAU PILSENER (West Germany)
Golden-hued. Malt and hop palate with firm hop finish.

★ ★ ★
RIVA 2000 LAGER BEER (Belgium)
Yellow golden. Fruity, hop-dominated nose and palate with background evidence of malt. Hoppy, somewhat metallic finish.

★
ROBIN HOOD CREAM ALE (United States)
From the vats of the Pittsburgh Brewing Company.

★
ROCK & ROLL BEER (United States)
From Saint Louis, Missouri.

★ ★ ★ ★
RODENBACH (Belgium)
Created in Roeselare, Flanders. Opaque, cherry-red hue topped with tannish cream foam. Distinctive sour-sweet nose and palate with hints of oak, caramel, cherries and lactic acid. Heady. Astringent but pleasant aftertaste.

★
ROLAND LIGHT (West Germany)
Low-calorie (96) beer. Brewed in Bremen by the Beck's people. Mild-mannered, but still has more character than typical American low-cal beers.

★
ROLLING ROCK (United States)
Produced by Latrobe Brewing Company in Pennsylvania.

ROLLING ROCK "LIGHT" BEER (United States)
From Latrobe, Pennsylvania. A milder version of the already mild Rolling Rock.

ROYAL BRAND BEER
See HOLLAND BRAND BEER.

★ ★ ★
ROYAL DUTCH LAGER BEER (Holland)
Golden-hued beer with a fruity, malt-hop nose. Sweet, somewhat oily palate. Citrus peel aftertaste.

★ ★
RUDDLES BITTER (England)
Amber-hued. Cream-colored head. Gassy, undeveloped palate.

★ ★ ★
RUDDLES COUNTY (England)
Amber liquid. Cream-colored head. Tart-bitter palate with fruity support extends from foretaste to finish.

★ ★ ★
SAGRES (Portugal)
From the Algarve region on the southern coast of Portugal. Amber hued. Malty nose and palate that finish pleasantly with hops.

★ ★ ★
SAGRES DARK (Portugal)
Chocolate cream head over deep reddish black brew. Bittersweet roasted malt character obvious in nose, stronger on palate and lingers in aftertaste. A little on the thin side for a dark beer.

★ ★
SAILER PILS (West Germany)
Amber-colored brew. Metallic hop finish is chief characteristic.

★ ★ ★
SAILER WEISSE (West Germany)
A wheat beer brewed in Martoberdorf, southern Bavaria. Pale yellow-gold hue. Gargantuan off-white head. Yeasty, sourish malt-wheat nose. Flavor not as complex as scent suggests.

★ ★ ★
SAILER WEISSE WITH YEAST (West Germany)
Wheat beer. Pale golden hue. Substantial head. Yeast dominates nose and palate.

ST. DAVID'S PORTER (Wales)
See FELINFOEL ST. DAVID'S PORTER.

ST. EDMUND SPECIAL PALE ALE (England)
See GREENE KING ST. EDMUND SPECIAL PALE ALE.

★ ★ ★
ST. PAULI GIRL DARK BEER (West Germany)
Brewed in Bremen especially for the American market by the makers of Beck's. Tiny bead. Semiopaque, reddish brown hue. Semisweet malty aroma and flavor partially balanced with dry hops. Medium full-bodied.

★ ★ ★ ★
ST. PAULI GIRL LIGHT BEER (West Germany)
A Bremener-Hamburger-style pale lager (not a low-calorie light beer). As with the dark St. Pauli Girl, this Bremen-brewed beer is custom-made for the U.S. market by the Beck's people. Similar to Beck's Light.

★ ★ ★ ★
ST. SIXTUS ABT BELGIUM ABBEY ALE (Belgium)
A Trappist ale. Expansive tan head. Opaque, deep ruby colored. Generous fruity nose. Bittersweet roasted malt palate with long candy sugar finish. Full-bodied. Alcoholic strength exceeds 10% by weight.

SALVATOR (West Germany)
See PAULANER SALVATOR.

★ ★ ★
SAMICHLAUS DARK BIER (Switzerland)
Translates as "Santa Claus." Produced by Brauerei Hurlimann in Zurich. Alcoholic content is 14% making this beer one of the strongest if not the strongest in the world. Unfortunately, this headiness overwhelms many of the other sensory attributes in the nose and palate. The tannish head is amazingly short-lived. Hue is deep, orangey ruby.

★ ★ ★
SAMICHLAUS PALE BIER (Switzerland)

Like its sister brew (see above), its 14 percent alcoholic content hogs the show. It also has a remarkably short-lived head. Its deep coppery orange liquid has commendable radiance.

★ ★ ★ ★
SAMUEL ADAMS BOSTON LAGER (United States)

Brewed in Pittsburgh, but marketed out of Boston. (However, plans are afoot to build a brewery in Greater Boston.) Dense, tannish cream head. Deep golden hue. Sweetish, fruity malt and nose. Hops speak boldy but properly in the midtaste and finish.

★ ★ ★ ★ ★
SAMUEL SMITH'S NUT BROWN ALE (England)

Brewed in Tadcaster, Yorkshire. Magnificent creamy tan head crowns the translucent reddish brown liquid. Nutty nose and palate, as the name promises. Superb hop-malt balance. Slightly sweeter than sister brew, Old Pale Ale. Luscious finish. (Note: Brewery affectionately called "Sam Smith's" by locals.)

★ ★ ★ ★ ★
SAMUEL SMITH'S OATMEAL STOUT (England)

Opaque, ruby-brown color. Large, creamy chocolate head. Complex yet smooth roasted malt nose and palate with sweetish undercurrents. Mouthfilling sensation. Full-bodied. Long finish.

★ ★ ★ ★ ★
SAMUEL SMITH'S OLD BREWERY PALE ALE (England)

Crafted in Tadcaster, Yorkshire. Crystalline, coppery orange liquid topped by a dense tannish cream head. Clean, fruity malted nose and flavor—beautifully balanced. Faintly sweet but still drier than sister brew, Nut Brown Ale. Full-bodied. Pleasing hoppy and burnt malt aftertaste.

★ ★ ★ ★ ★
SAMUEL SMITH'S TADDY PORTER (England)
Opaque ruby-brown hue with an ample, creamy tan head. Smooth, bittersweet nose and palate of amazing complexity. full-bodied. Ethereal finish with bitter infrastructure.

★ ★ ★
SAN MIGUEL BEER (Philippines)
From Manila. Liquid is yellow golden. Nose and palate are fruity with a hoppy background.

★ ★ ★
SAN MIGUEL DARK BEER (Philippines)
Though San Miguel brews its product in many countries, the version imported to the United States is produced in Manila. Opaque, reddish brown-black. Rich malty nose with a bittersweet roasted malt palate. Medium-full body.

★ ★
SAPPORO DRAFT BEER (Japan)
Not a genuine draft beer. Brewed in Tokyo. Golden hue. Big bubbles. Somewhat gassy. Relatively thin palate.

★ ★ ★
SAPPORO LAGER BEER (Japan)
Golden liquid. Nose and taste have earthy edge.

★ ★
SARANAC ALL MALT 1888 LAGER (United States)
Brewed by F.X. Matt Brewing Company in Utica, New York. Cream-hued head. Golden body. Malty nose. Moderate gassiness in mouthfeel.

★ ★ ★ ★
SCALDIS (Belgium)
Deep orange liquid topped with large tannish cream head. Earthy, sweet-malt nose and palate. Full-bodied with obvious potency. Sprightly mouthfeel. Lingering bittersweet hop finish.

★ ★
SCANDIA GOLD (Denmark)
International-style pale lager brewed in Copenhagen. Deep gold color. Active carbonation. Unbalanced; hops insufficient to offset the semisweet taste and finish.

★
SCHAEFER (United States)
Brewed in Pennsylvania's Lehigh Valley. Schaefer's flavor profile was once more interesting.

★
SCHAEFER CREAM ALE (United States)
A product of the F&M Schaefer Brewing Company, a subsidiary of Stroh.

SCHAEFER LIGHT LAGER BEER (United States)
A low-calorie light beer.

★ ★ ★
SCHELL'S EXPORT (United States)
Made by the August Schell brewery in New Ulm, Minnesota. Yellow golden. Malty but hop-dominated nose and palate.

SCHELL WEISS BEER (United States)
See AUGUST SCHELL WEISS BEER.

★ ★
SCHILD BRAU PILS (United States)
Produced by Millstream Brewing Company in Amana, Iowa. Creamy tan head. Copper hue. Bittersweet notes throughout flavor profile. Slight fizziness in finish.

★
SCHLITZ (United States)
"The beer that made Milwaukee famous" is now brewed in several locations, but not in Milwaukee. Schiltz has become part of the Stroh brewing family. Its quality has slipped dramatically over recent decades.

★
SCHLITZ MALT LIQUOR (United States)
Heady and obvious sensory profile without any subtlety. "The bull" is now in the corral of the Stroh brewing family.

★
SCHMIDT BEER (United States)
American-style pale lager now under the auspices of Heileman. This Saint Paul, Minnesota brew is not to be confused with Schmidt's of Philadelphia.

SCHMIDT LIGHT (United States)

★
SCHMIDT'S BAVARIAN BEER (United States)
It doesn't taste like any beer in Bavaria. Brewed in Philadelphia.

★
SCHMIDT'S BEER (United States)
American-style pale lager brewed by Schmidt's of Philadelphia

(not to be confused with the Schmidt brand brewed in Minnesota). Pale yellow hue. Mild, sweet and fizzy. Scant aftertaste. Better in the old days.

★ ★
SCHMIDT'S BOCK BEER (United States)
From Philadelphia. Translucent, reddish brown liquid that sports a light tan head. Spicy chocolate nose. Flavor is caramelized bitter chocolate. Somewhat thin-bodied for a bock beer.

SCHMIDT'S LIGHT BEER (United States)
A low-calorie light beer brewed in Philadelphia and Cleveland.

★
SCHOENLING BEER (United States)
A regional brew from Cincinnati, Ohio.

★ ★ ★
SCHUTZ BIERE D'ALSACE (France)
Brewed in Schiltigheim. Pale gold color. Tanginess revealed in midtaste and finish.

★ ★ ★
SCHUTZENBURGER JUBILATOR (France)
Pale gold. Sweet-tart malty nose and palate. Don't be misled by the "ator" suffix—this brew is not a Dopplebock, neither is it heady or full-bodied.

SCHWEIZERHOFBRAU (West Germany)
See KULMBACHER SCHWEIZERHOFBRAU.

★
SCOTCH BUY BEER (United States)
A budget-priced beer produced by Falstaff.

★
SCOTTISH PRIDE (Scotland)
Better-than-average low-calorie light beer.

★ ★ ★
SEPTANTE 5 (France)
Amber-hued. Cream-colored head. Palate has bittersweet chocolate undertones. Fizzy mouthfeel.

★ ★ ★
SEPTANTE ROUGE (France)
Amber-colored liquid. Tannish cream head. Exhibits a hint of bittersweeet chocolate flavor.

★ ★ ★
SEPTANTE VERTE (France)
Blond-gold hue. Nose and palate exhibit obvious tartness. Quick finish.

★ ★
SHANGHAI BEER (People's Republic of China)
Sweet-sour grainy nose and palate with a hoppy aftertaste. The Shanghai available in the U.S. is superior to local brews tasted in Shanghai.

★ ★ ★
SHEAF STOUT (Australia)
Made in the beautiful city of Sydney. Large, dense, dark tan head. Opaque, brownish black hue. Heady, roasted malt nose. Sweet, bitter, malt-hop palate. Scorched, slightly cloying caramel candy finish. Not as full-bodied as a stout should be.

★
SHINER PREMIUM (United States)
A Texas beer made by the Spoetzl Brewery.

★ ★ ★

SHULTHEISS ORIGINAL BERLINER WEISSE (West Germany)

A wheat beer fashioned in Berlin. Hazy liquid due to yeast. Enormous white head. Yeasty, berrylike sweet-and-sour nose reminiscent of pickle relish. Pronounced astringent-tart palate and finish.

★ ★ ★ ★

SIERRA NEVADA BIGFOOT ALE (United States)

Barleywine-style brew vatted in Chico, California. Semiopaque reddish brown hue. Generous, dense head. Obvious pineapple nose. Sweetish, scorched malt flavor. Heady. Prolonged aftertaste.

★ ★ ★ ★ ★

SIERRA NEVADA CELEBRATION ALE (United States)

A Christmas beer crafted in a small northern California brewery. Its profile changes slightly year to year, but this brew typically has an amber-hued body and huge, dense tannish cream head. Surprisingly genteel considering its headiness, bittersweet nose and roasted malt palate.

★ ★ ★ ★

SIERRA NEVADA PALE ALE (United States)

From Chico, California. Thick, pale tan head. Deep honey amber colored. Hazy because it is bottle conditioned. Rich, fruity, malt-hop aroma. Firm hoppy palate and aftertaste that perfectly balances the brew's slight sweetness.

★ ★ ★ ★ ★

SIERRA NEVADA PORTER (United States)

Tan head over a brew that is opaque and brownish black. Fruity, berrylike malty nose. Muscular, bittersweet palate with emphatic hop finish. full-bodied.

★ ★ ★ ★ ★
SIERRA NEVADA STOUT (United States)

Sizable, dense, and remarkably long lasting dark tan head that clings to a spoon almost like batter. Brownish black opaque liquid. Roasted malt nose with an earthy accent. Bittersweet roasted malt palate and aftertaste. Slightly sweeter and less bitter than Guinness Extra Stout (q.v.).

★ ★ ★ ★
SIERRA NEVADA SUMMERFEST BEER (United States)

Brewed in northern California in Chico, near Sacramento. Off-white head. Golden hued. Malty nose with hop and sweet notes. Pleasant, refreshing tartness from midtaste through finish.

★ ★ ★
SIGNATURE (United States)

Produced by The Stroh Brewery Company. The golden liquid emanates a malty nose with hops aromatic in the background. Clean, malty palate with a hoppy superstructure followed by a pleasant hoppy aftertaste. Medium to medium-full-bodied.

★ ★ ★
SIMPATICO BEER (West Germany)

A Bamberg-brewed beer. Pale gold liquid. Malt outplays the hop flavor. Slight bite in aftertaste. Sold in gimmicky black-painted bottle.

★ ★
SINGHA LAGER BEER (Thailand)

Brewed in Bangkok. Yellow gold hue. Sweet fragrant aroma. Fruity taste. Hoppy finish.

★ ★ ★ ★
1664 DE KRONENBOURG (France)

Brewed in Alsace. Higher alcoholic content, fuller-bodied and deeper-flavored than regular Kronenbourg.

★ ★ ★ ★
SNAKE RIVER AMBER LAGER (United States)
Brewed and bottled in Caldwell, Idaho. Dense, creamy tan head. Amber liquid. Fruity malty nose with sweet-sour accent. Malty palate with cidery notes.

★
SOL ESPECIAL (Mexico)
Manufactured in Orizaba. Grainy, skimpy flavor. Slightly gassy palate. Short-lived head.

★
SOUTH PACIFIC EXPORT LAGER (Papua New Guinea)
Golden-hued international-style pale lager. Nose and palate have tangy backdrop. Short-lived head.

★ ★
SPARTAN LAGER EXPORT (Greece)
An international-style pale lager. Amber hued. Mild fruity nose with some bite in the finish.

★ ★ ★
SPATEN CLUB-WEISSE (West Germany)
Brewed in Munich. Inviting rich amber hue that is uncharacteristically brilliant for a wheat beer. Gargantuan head. Fresh malty, lemony aroma, though somewhat bland in taste. A slice of lemon dropped through the foam makes it a refreshing summer drink.

★ ★ ★ ★
SPATEN DOPPELSPATEN OPTIMATOR (West Germany)
A Doppelbock beer brewed in Munich. Dark reddish copper. Very sweet roasted malt nose and flavor with a prolonged sweet finish. Medium full-bodied.

★ ★ ★ ★
SPATENGOLD (West Germany)
Brewed in Munich. Pale golden. Milder and gassier than Spaten Pils, but still a worthy brew.

★ ★ ★ ★
SPATEN MUNICH LIGHT BEER (West Germany)
Munich pale lager (*helles*). Beautiful golden hue. Malty flavor partially balanced with clean hop accent. Lingering finish.

★ ★ ★ ★
SPATEN PILS (West Germany)
Produced by Spaten, one of Munich's leading breweries. Golden hue. Complex palate with hoppy finish.

★ ★ ★ ★
SPATEN UR-MÄRZEN OKTOBERFEST BEER (West Germany)
Deep amber with a gorgeous dense, pale tawny head. Toasted nut aroma. Sweet with a bitter background from roasted malt. Potent and full-bodied.

★ ★
STAG (United States)
American-style pale lager with an overall mellow character save for a touch of crisp tartness. A brand of the Heileman empire.

★ ★ ★ ★
STAUDER (West Germany)
Brewed in Essen. Golden yellow tone. Fruity nose. Slightly sweet yet crisp, hop-dominated flavor.

★ ★
STEFFL EXPORT LAGER (Austria)
Brewed in Vienna. Golden with a citric nose and a sweet-sour palate.

★ ★ ★
STEFFL VIENNA LAGER BEER (Austria)
A Viennese beer with a golden hue. Malty nose and palate. Mild hop aftertaste.

STEG LIGHT (United States)
From Wilkes-Barre, Pennsylvania.

★
STEGMAIER GOLD MEDAL BEER (United States)
Produced in Wilkes-Barre, Pennsylvania.

★
STEINHAUS (United States)
American-style pale lager made by the August Schell brewery in New Ulm, Minnesota.

★ ★ ★ ★
STEINHÄUSER BIER (West Germany)
An international-style pale lager custom-brewed in Frankfurt for the American market. Slightly sweet nose and palate.

★ ★ ★
STEINLAGER (New Zealand)
International-style pale lager. Golden yellow hue. Ample off-white head. Sweet foretaste that gives way to a noticeable biting midtaste with honeylike undertones. Fair lace.

★ ★ ★
STELLA ARTOIS (Belgium)
An international-style pale lager brewed in Leuven, Belgium. Gold hue. Malt and hops in balance in both nose and palate.

★ ★
STERLING BEER (United States)
American-style pale lager. Gold hue. Uncomplex but clean, soothing character.

★ ★ ★ ★
STERN PREMIUM (West Germany)
International-style pale lager brewed in Essen. Amber golden. Fruity, somewhat citrus peel nose and palate with a toasted malt veil.

★ ★ ★
STINGO CREAM STOUT (England)
Dense, creamy chocolate brown head. Deep, sweetish roasted malt nose and palate with smoky undertones.

★ ★ ★ ★
STINGO DARK ALE (England)
Brewed in London. Dense, deep tan rocky head. Reddish brown opaque liquid. Rich peachy, earthy nose—complex. Creamy mouthfeel counterpointed by bittersweet scorched malt flavor. Full-bodied. Lengthy finish with hoppy accent.

★
STONEY'S BEER (United States)
A product of the Jones brewery located in Smithton, Pennsylvania.

★
STONEY'S LIGHT (United States)
Brewed by Jones Brewing Company in Smithton, Pennsylvania. Off-white head. Yellow-gold hue. Sweetish grainy-malt flavor profile. Thin-bodied. Short finish.

★ ★ ★ ★
STRASBRAU PILSENER (West Germany)
Produced by Euler in Wetzlar. Golden liquid emanates a hoppy, malty nose. Pleasantly sharp hoppy palate.

★ ★ ★
STRAUB BEER (United States)
A regional favorite around St. Marys, Pennsylvania. Pale yellow-gold. Grainy malt nose. Malty palate with a hop balance. Slightly smoky-woody hop aftertaste.

★
STROH LIGHT (United States)
A low-calorie light beer. Stroh's entry into the light beer market displays more character than the typical American low-calorie beer.

★ ★
STROH'S BOHEMIAN STYLE BEER (United States)
This "fire-brewed" beer is gold in color and has a somewhat earthy nose. Pleasant, but lacks character in the midtaste. Crisp, somewhat gassy palate.

★ ★ ★
STROH'S OWN BOCK BEER (United States)
Translucent coppery brown liquid topped by a creamy tan head. Sweetish, roasted malt nose. Bittersweet, lingering malt palate balanced with hops.

SUFFOLK DARK ENGLISH ALE (England)
See GREENE KING SUFFOLK DARK ENGLISH ALE.

★ ★
SUMMIT AMBER BEER (United States)
Brewed in Dunkirk, New York. Amber head. Sweetish nose with bitter malt palate.

★
SUN LIK BEER (Hong Kong)
Produced and bottled by Hong Kong Brewery Limited.

★ ★
SUNTORY DRAFT BEER (Japan)
Brewed in Osaka and Tokyo. A pseudo-draft beer with a personality too sweet, bland and gassy to earn a third star.

★ ★ ★
SUPERIOR (Mexico)
Golden hued with an earthy nose and rich mouthfeel. Because of its balance and relative depth of character, Superior is indeed superior to the other Mexican pale lagers (but not to the amber-hued Dos Equis (XX) Beer).

★
SWAN LAGER EXPORT (Australia)
An international-style pale lager from Perth in western Australia.

★ ★ ★
SWINKELS (Holland)
Brewed in Lieshout. Brass-tinged gold color. A bit sweeter than traditional Dutch brews, but hops help mitigate that shortcoming.

★
TAIWAN BEER (Taiwan)
Brewed in Taipei by the Taiwan Tobacco & Wine Monopoly Bureau. Not a particularly enticing name.

★ ★
TAJ MAHAL LAGER BEER (India)
A Calcutta-brewed international-style pale lager. Grainy, floral nose with earthy background note. Slight tooth-coating metallic bite.

TARTAN ALE (Scotland)
See McEWAN'S TARTAN ALE.

★ ★
TASMANIAN LAGER BEER (Australia)
Manufactured in Hobart, the capital of the island of Tasmania. Pale amber. Tropical fruit (papayalike) nose. Hops come through on the palate.

★
TECATE (Mexico)
Produced by the makers of Carta Blanca. Its popularity outstrips its quality.

★
TEXAS PRIDE EXTRA LIGHT LAGER (United States)
Not a low-calorie light beer. Made in San Antonio by Pearl Brewing Company.

TEXAS PRIDE LITE (United States)
A low-calorie light beer.

★ ★ ★
THEAKSTON BEST BITTER ALE (England)
Brewed in Masham. Amber hue. Large, cream-colored head. Trace of raw hops in scent and taste. Short finish for a bitter ale.

★ ★ ★
"33" EXPORT (France)
International-style pale lager brewed in Paris. Deep amber. Citrus peel and faint malt in the nose. Somewhat heady palate with tart finish.

★ ★ ★
"33" EXTRA DRY (France)
Produced in Paris. Faint roasted malt nose. Tart, malt-top palate with noticeable alcohol. Drier, as its name implies, than the "33" Export.

★ ★ ★ ★
THOUSAND OAKS GOLDEN BEAR (United States)
Created in a Berkeley, California boutique brewery. Opaque garnet-brown hue. Cream-tan head. Sweetish pineapple scent and flavor notes with a noticeable bitter epilogue.

★ ★ ★ ★
THOUSAND OAKS GOLDEN GATE MALT LIQUOR (United States)
A California boutique brewery product. Pale cream head. Malty nose evinces headiness. Detectable scorched, smoked malt flavor.

★ ★ ★ ★
THOUSAND OAKS LAGER (United States)
From the San Francisco Bay area. Honey-gold liquid is hazy because beer is bottle-conditioned. Rich, intensely malty nose and flavor. Finish could be a trifle longer.

★ ★ ★
THREE HORSES BRAND PILSENER (Holland)
International-style pale lager. Amber-hued brew that emanates a fresh, faintly yeasty nose. Tart, malty hop palate with a touch of saltiness in the finish.

★ ★
TIGER HEAD ALE (United States)
Brewed by C. Schmidt & Sons. Orange-tinged amber. Peachy nose. Tangy hop palate and finish.

★
TIGER LAGER BEER (Singapore)
Pale gold hue. Relatively bland. Hints of tropical fruits in nose and palate. Low-keyed lemon tartness in finish.

★ ★
TIJUCA (Brazil)
Brewed in Belem near where the Amazon flows into the Atlantic. Gold hue. Citric-sour underpinning. Hint of astringency in finish.

★ ★ ★ ★
TOLLY ORIGINAL ALE (England)
Brewed in Suffolk. Generous amber-tinged creamy head. Copper-hued. Pronounced hoppy nose and palate. Lengthy finish.

★
TOOHEY'S LAGER BEER (Australia)
Brewed in New South Wales. Amber-gold. Sweetish, slightly tart nose, palate and finish.

TOOTHS SHEAF STOUT (Australia)
See SHEAF STOUT.

★
TOPA'ZIO (Portugal)
Produced in Coimbra, in northern Portugal. Pale gold brew. Small and short-lived head. Touch of citric sourness in both nose and palate.

★
TOP HAT BEER (United States)
Produced by the Schoenling Brewing Company in Cincinnati, Ohio.

★ ★
TRAPPER BEER (Canada)
Imported from Red Deer, Alberta. Pale yellow golden. Grainy malt nose and palate with sweet-tart accent.

★ ★
TRES EQUIS (XXX) (Mexico)
Differs from its sibling brew, Dos Equis (XX) Beer (q.v.), in several prominent ways. Tres Equis is fuller-bodied, sweeter, fuller-flavored and more potent. Of the two, Dos Equis (XX) Beer is better.

TRIPEL ABBEY BEER (Belgium)
See AFFLIGEM TRIPEL ABBEY BEER.

★
TROPICAL EXPORT (Canary Islands)
Pale international-style lager brewed in Las Palmas. Golden-hued. Grainy nose. Thin palate.

★ ★
TSINGTAO BEER (People's Republic of China)
Manufactured in Tsingtao. Pale golden hue. Sweet-tangy, grainy aroma and taste. This imported version is better than the Tsingtaos I've sampled in various cities in China.

★ ★
TUBORG BEER (United States)
A product of the G. Heileman Brewing Company. Milder, sweeter and gassier than the original brewed-in-Denmark version which rates four stars.

★
TUBORG DELUXE DARK (United States)
Part of the Heileman Brewing empire.

★ ★ ★ ★
TUCHER HEFE WEIZEN (West Germany)
A wheat beer produced in Nürnberg. Gold hue that is hazy, as name implies (*hefe* means that the beer still contains yeast). Nose has faint roasted malt and hop tones with obvious yeastiness.

★ ★ ★ ★
TUCHER WEIZEN (West Germany)
Golden liquid wheat beer. Lightly roasted, malty nose and palate with some hops. Unlike the Tucher Hefe Weizen (see above), this product does not have yeast sediment.

★ ★
ULMER BEER (United States)
Made by the August Schell brewery in New Ulm, Minnesota. Malty nose and palate, but generally unassuming.

ULTBANERISCHES WEISSBIER (West Germany)
See PAULANER ULTBANERISCHES WEISSBIER.

ULT-MÜNCHNER DUNKEL (West Germany)
See PAULANER ULT-MÜNCHNER DUNKEL.

UR-MARZEN OKTOBERFEST BEER (West Germany)
See SPATEN UR-MÄRZEN OKTOBERFEST BEER.

URTYP 1634 (West Germany)
See PAULANER URTYP 1634.

★ ★
UTICA CLUB CREAM ALE (United States)
Produced by West End Brewing of Utica, New York. The liquid is deep golden and emanates a hoppy nose. Sweetish grain-malt-hop flavor.

UTICA CLUB LIGHT BEER (United States)

A low-calorie light beer.

UTICA CLUB PILSENER (United States)

American-style pale lager produced in Utica, New York by the West End Brewing Company.

VALLEY FORGE OLD TAVERN BEER (United States)

A regional brew produced by Schmidt's in their Philadelphia plant.

VAUX DOUBLE MAXIM BROWN ALE (England)

Brewed in Sunderland, Durham. Dense, expansive tan head supported by translucent orange-amber liquid. Fruity hop and roasted malt aroma. Caramelized roasted malt palate backed by bitterness. Medium full-bodied. Prolonged finale.

★ ★ ★ ★

VIENNA LAGER BEER (United States)

Brewed by Vienna Brewery in Eau Claire, Wisconsin. Semi-dense, tan-cream head. Copper-amber hue. Rich malty nose and palate with obvious fruity-caramelized notes. Hops make statement, especially in finish.

WALTER'S (United States)

Produced by the Walter Brewing Company of Eau Claire, Wisconsin.

WALTER'S LIGHT (United States)

As low-calorie light beers go, this has more character than the average.

★ ★
WALTER'S SPECIAL BEER (United States)
Yellow golden with a grainy malt nose. Crisp palate that has a trace of roasted peanuts in the background.

★ ★ ★
WARSTEINER PREMIUM VERUM (West Germany)
Golden-hued brew with a citric-malt nose. Malt-hop palate with a metallic hop finish.

★ ★ ★ ★
WATNEYS BEER (England)
Copper-colored liquid sports a dense, creamy tan head. Subdued, sweet malt nose. Velvety caramel candy taste, but not cloyingly so. Medium full-bodied. Good lace. Long-lived head.

★
WEBER (United States)
American-style lager from the vats of the Dubuque Star brewery in Iowa.

WEINHARD BAVARIAN DARK BEER (United States)
See BLITZ WEINHARD BAVARIAN DARK BEER.

★ ★ ★
WEINHARD'S PREMIUM LIGHT ALE (United States)
Brewed in Portland, Oregon by Blitz-Weinhard. Golden-hued. Smooth, slightly sweet malty nose and palate. Could use more hops.

WEIZENKRONE (West Germany)
See DINKELACKER WEIZENKRONE.

★ ★ ★ ★
WESTFALEN PILS (West Germany)
Brewed in Lippstadt, Westphalia. Malt base. Light suggestion of mealiness.

★
WESTERN BEER (United States)
An American-style pale lager made by the Cold Spring Brewing Company in Minnesota.

★ ★ ★ ★
WHITBREAD ALE (England)
Splendid head and coppery color. Spicy-sweet apple aroma. Austere hop flavor and finish.

★ ★
WHITE LABEL (United States)
Produced by the Cold Spring Brewing Company in Minnesota. Apple-malt nose. Hop-malt infused palate.

★ ★ ★ ★
WICKÜLER PILSENER (West Germany)
Pale gold hue. Malty palate, hop finish. Crisp mouthfeel.

★ ★
WIEDEMANN BOHEMIAN SPECIAL (United States)
American-style pale lager that is part of the Heileman empire. Brewed in Newport, Kentucky. Pale yellow hue. Slightly sweet nose. Unassertive palate.

★
WILD MUSTANG MALT LIQUOR (United States)
Produced by the Pittsburgh Brewing Company in Pittsburgh, Pennsylvania.

★
WINDJAMMER LUSTY LAGER (United States)
Brewed in upstate New York. Pale gold liquid. Bleached white head. Slightly sweet, grainy malt nose and palate with curious bitter chalky finish.

★ ★
WISCONSIN CLUB (United States)
A product of Huber Brewing in Wisconsin. Amber-gold. Scent has an earthy echo. Smooth, semiunctuous palate with a hoppy aftertaste.

★ ★ ★ ★
WITTEKOP BIERE BLANCHE (Belgium)
Brewed in Dentergem, near Ghent. Pale yellow hue. Yeasty haze due to second fermentation in bottle. Giant white head. Citric-peel scent and flavor. Especially refreshing during warm months.

★ ★ ★ ★
WÖLFBRÄU (West Germany)
Vatted in Osnabruck. Crisp, hop-malt palate, but the beer has less verve than the typical northern German brews.

★ ★ ★
WREXHAM LAGER BEER (Wales)
Brewed in Wrexham, near the English border. Yellow-gold hue. Off-white head. Tart-edged hoppy malt nose and palate. Finish falls off quickly for a British lager.

★ ★ ★ ★
WÜRZBURGER HOFBRÄU BAVARIAN BEER (West Germany)
Pale yellow-gold color. Rich, malty nose and palate supported by hops. Crisp palate.

★ ★ ★ ★
WÜRZBURGER HOFBRÄU BAVARIAN DARK BEER (West Germany)

Semiopaque, ruby-orange-tinted brown hue. Tannish cream head. Roasted malt in both scent and taste. Some tart-bitterness in finish.

★ ★ ★ ★
WÜRZBURGER HOFBRÄU BAVARIAN HOLIDAY BEER (West Germany)

Opaque ruby-brown liquid topped with cream-tan head. Bittersweet malt nose and palate. Bitter note in finish. Heady.

★ ★ ★ ★
WÜRZBURGER HOFBRÄU MAY BOK (West Germany)

Gold-hued bock beer. Off-white head with touch of tan. Malty nose and palate have sweet-tart underpinning. Long, slightly bitter, metallic hoppy finish.

★ ★ ★ ★
WÜRZBURGER HOFBRÄU OCTOBERFEST-BEER (West Germany)

Brewed in Bavaria. Creamy tan head floats on light copper-hued brew. Rich, heady, sweetish, malty nose and palate. Hops in background.

★ ★ ★ ★
X-PERT HOLLAND BEER (Holland)

Orange-amber hue with greenish copper tinge. Full, fruity malt nose. Tangy hop finish.

XXX ALE (United States)

See BALLANTINE XXX ALE.

★
YACHT CLUB BEER (United States)
A product of C. Schmidt & Sons.

★
YUCHUAN (China)
An international-style pale lager brewed in the People's Republic of China.

★ ★
YUENGLING & SON PREMIUM BEER (United States)
Pale gold liquid. Sweetish, pine forest nose. Tart and slightly gassy with a citric aftertaste.

★ ★ ★ ★
YUENGLING DARK PORTER BREW (United States)
Crafted in Pottsville, Pennsylvania by America's oldest extant brewery. Opaque brown liquid with a reddish tinge. Dark beige head. Roasted malt nose. Caramelized malt taste. Creamy mouthfeel.

★ ★
YUKON CANADIAN CREAM ALE (Canada)
Produced by the Pacific Western Brewing Company in Vancouver, British Columbia. Pale yellow-gold brew. Sweetish, grainy nose and palate.

★
YUKON GOLD CANADIAN LAGER BEER (Canada)
Manufactured in British Columbia. Pale yellow golden liquid emanates a fruity aroma. Watery palate.

★ ★ ★
ZIPFER URTYPE LAGER BEER (Austria)
Pale amber-gold. Malty nose. Hop-dominated palate and finish.

★ ★ ★
ZYWIEC (Poland)
Brewed in the town of Zywiec. Honey golden. A bit hoppier than the standard Polish import.

PART FIVE

HOW BEER IS MADE

THE INGREDIENTS

Creating a brew is like concocting a stew. The outcome will be only as good as the quality of your ingredients.

To make beer, you need a fermentable cereal grain (barley, for instance), a fermenting agent (yeast) and water. Optional, though quite desirable, is a flavoring and preserving agent like hops. Also optional though undesirable are artificial flavors and colors, carbonic injection, foam stabilizers and chemical preservatives. Most American beers are laden with these additives, one brand allegedly has 59.

The most famous beer law is the Rheinheitsgebot, the Bavarian purity decree of 1516 which is still enforced in Germany for domestically consumed brews. Several other European countries, including Switzerland, have adopted it as well. Essentially, the wording, combined with the modern interpretation of this historic document, mandates that beer can be made with only four ingredients: barley (plus wheat in the case of wheat beers), hops, yeast and water. Under no circumstances can the brewer use adjuncts such as corn or rice, or chemical additives. The Rheinheitsgebot doesn't cover the German beer we import, but most of the quality brewers nonetheless abide by it for all their products.

Barley and Adjuncts

Beer can be made from any cereal grain: barley, corn, wheat, rice, oats or rye. I've even helped make a native-brewed millet beer in a small Zambian village in Africa.

The cereal grain contributes color, sweetness, body, protein, carbohydrates, vitamins and minerals. Most important of all, it provides the starch that is converted into sugar by means of malting. This sugar, in turn, is transformed into alcohol and carbon dioxide by means of fermentation.

197

Barley is by far the best cereal grain for making beer. It gives brew a fuller body and a richer, more invitingly complex nose and flavor than its rival. Why then do so many brewers substitute adjuncts (nonbarley cereal grains) such as corn or rice for the barley? Adjuncts are cheaper and make the brewing process less troublesome and time-consuming. They also produce a lighter beer with less character, the type many Americans prefer.

Adjuncts—with the exception of wheat—produce skimpy, short-lived heads. Brewers then overcome this handicap with the use of foaming agents and head stabilizers.

There are three basic types of barley: the two-, four- and six-row varieties. This classification refers to the number of rows of barleycorns on each of the seed-bearing spikes of the plant. Two-row barley makes the finest beer. Six-row barley gives beer a coarser taste but is often used in ordinary brands because it is cheaper than two-row. Four-row barley is the least used and most undesirable.

Before the barley can be fermented, it must be malted. The barley is moistened, partially sprouted and then kiln dried to halt the germination process which has converted some of the starch into sugar. The more the barley is roasted during this drying step, the sweeter and deeper hued the beer will be. Well-roasted barley will also give beer a bitter note. Black Patent, the most roasted of all the barley malts, can give a brew a pleasingly sharp, burnt palate, as in Guinness.

Some brewers make their beers with a combination of roasted unmalted barley and roasted malted barley. Guinness is one of them.

The best brews are made with unadulterated malt. Lesser brews are often made in whole or in part with commercial malt extract, a convenience product which has been processed into powder or syrup before being shipped to the brewer. This extra processing step robs malt of much of its aromatic and flavor potential.

Hops

Humulus lupulus may sound like the name of an obscure Roman emperor, but it is the Latin botanical name for the hop plant, a member of the nettle family and a relative of marijuana. Think of a tiny, yellowish green soft-leaved pine cone measuring an inch or so in length and you will have a rough idea of what the female hop flower looks like as it hangs from the climbing hop vine.

Only the flower from the female plant is used in making brew. In many European countries, the cultivation of the male plant is prohibited to prevent possible fertilization of the female flower which could affect the quality of the brew. The female plants do not need sex to reproduce because the plants are propagated by cuttings, not seeds. Technically, today's commercially grown hop plants are clones.

The dry, tangy bitterness of hops helps balance the natural sweetness of the malt and piques the appetite. Yet, hop-infused beers have been prevalent only in the last few centuries. Prior to that, brew was customarily flavored with different seasoning agents, including herbs, spices, berries and a wide assortment of nonhop flowers.

I've seen hops growing in temperate climates throughout the world. Perhaps the five most celebrated hop-growing areas are Bohemia in Czechoslovakia, Bavaria in West Germany, Kent in England, Tasmania in Australia and the Yakima Valley in Washington. All happen to be picturesque and well worth a detour.

Brewers can choose from a score of basic hop types, old-timers and new hybrids among them. The best-known varieties include:

HOP TYPE	ORIGINAL SOURCE	SENSORY CHARACTERISTICS
Brewer's Gold	England	distinctive sharp, acidic flavor
Cascade	United States	expansive aroma evocative of forests
Cluster	United States	mild, laid back scent and flavor
Fuggle	England	firm scent with spicy undertones
Goldings	England	slightly more subtle than Fuggle
Halletau	Germany	complex with above average bitterness
Northern Brewer	England	pronounced bitterness lends backbone to full- flavored brews
Saaz	Czecholslovakia	tangy with rich subtleties

Typically, brewers use a blend of hops. The exact Budweiser blend is a secret, but it is known that the brewmaster uses at least a dozen different varieties of hops. In this case, there is safety in numbers because if one hop type suddenly becomes unavailable due to a crop failure, its absence would not cause a beer-hall brawl among Bud's loyal fans.

Hops are added to the developing beer in at least two distinct batches. The first is added at the beginning of the boiling (brewing) step. This batch is called flavoring hops because its purpose is to flavor the brew. It will not do much for the aroma because the volatile ordorants escape into the air during the boiling process.

The final batch is incorporated at, or near the end of, the boiling step because the brewer wants to preserve the hop odorants for the drinker's nose. These hops are referred to as finishing or aromatic hops. Some varities—like Hallertau—are ideal flavoring hops. Others—like Cascade—perform best as finishing hops.

A few brewers add yet another round of hops after the brew is fermented. This technique, called "dry hopping," increases the aromatic quality of the brew.

Brewers can buy hops in several commercial forms. The best and most costly are minimally processed hop flowers or petals that have only been air dried. Highly processed hops include hop pellets (pulverized leaves pressed into tablets) and hop extract (hop resins and oils removed by a solvent). Both reduce purchasing, shipping, storage and processing costs at the expense of quality.

Yeast

Yeast are microscopic, single-cell, living organisms of the fungus family. From the brewer's point of view, this chlorophylless plant is classified into three basic categories:

CATEGORY	SPECIES
"bottom fermenting" yeast	*Saccharomyces uvarum*
"top fermenting" yeast	*Saccharomyces cerevisiae*
wild yeasts	*Saccharomyces candida* and other species

Each species if further subdivided into strains, each of which is capable of giving beer a distinctive taste. Consequently, a brewery must diligently safeguard the purity of its proprietary strain to insure that its loyal consumers get a consistent product. Should a wild or the wrongly cultured yeast strain (or certain bacteria) enter the brewery, it could attack the nascent brew, making it hazy and imparting off-odors and -flavors. Breweries must be regularly scrubbed and sterilized to keep them "hospital clean."

Fermentation takes place when the yeast (we hope the right strain) attacks the natural malt sugar, converting it into approximately equal parts of alcohol and carbon dioxide gas. At the end of the fermentation stage, the yeast is removed. A small quantity is kept as a starter for the next batch. The rest is sold as brewer's yeast, a by-product rich in protein and the various B-complex vitamins. It is used in human and animal diets as a food supplement and is a reputed blood purifier.

Water

Water to the brewer is more than H_2O. It is also the mineral salts dissolved in it. These compounds, particuarly calcium sulfate and magnesium sulfate, affect the character of the brew.

A water perfectly suited for one beer style is usually less than ideally suited for another style. Bass India Pale Ale is an exalted amber ale because, in part, it is made with Burton-on-Trent well water, which has an exceptionally high gypsum (calcium sulfate) content: 352 milligrams per liter. This hard water gives Burton ales their mouthcoating and mineral salt characteristics. In contrast, the liquid used to produce the legendary Pilsner Urquell is a semisoft water with a gypsum content of only 7 milligrams per liter. Bass India Pale Ale and Pilsner Urquell (a lager) would be lesser brews if they switched water sources.

In Tahiti, I have sampled several local brews, including Wahini ("woman") and Hinano ("girl"). These brews have distinctive flavors because they are made with fresh tropical rainwater that has surged down mineral-rich volcanic mountain peaks.

In the past, a superior brew could only be made if there was a nearby source of water ideally suited for the brewer's type of beer. Modern chemistry and technology has changed that. It is now possible to make a thoroughly decent brew out of water from muddy rivers, musty quagmires, polluted lakes, briny oceans and even fetid sewers if a brewer has no better alternative. Even the water taken from those heavily advertised cascading mountain streams and pristine springs usually benefits from treatment to adjust its mineral content and pH factor.

If necessary, the water is cleaned by ridding it of pathogenic microorganisms, toxic chemicals, excessive mineral salts and other unwanted compounds. It is then fortified with new compounds to bring its content of calcium and magnesium sulfates and other minerals up to the level best suited for the particular beer.

THE PROCESS

Do you know how commercial breweries manufacture their products? Few beer drinkers do. This is a pity because beer drinking is more enjoyable if you have at least a layperson's understanding of the process. This chapter gives you a thumbnail sketch.

There are nine basic steps: steeping, germinating, kilning, milling, mashing, boiling, fermenting, maturing and bottling. (See the accompanying schematic diagram.) Collectively, the commercial beer-making process can take anywhere from a couple of weeks to four months.

FIGURE 2

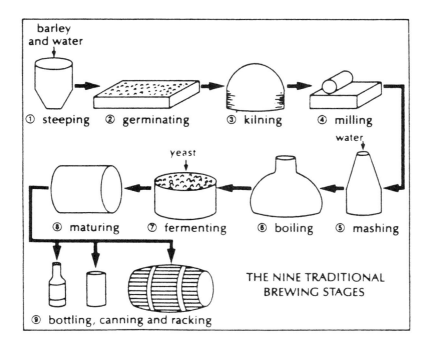

Stage One. Steeping. When the barley grains arrive at the brewery, they are dry and hard, like uncooked rice. The brewer thoroughly softens these grains by soaking them in water for about two days in the steeping tank.

Stage Two. Germinating (Malting). The soaked barley grains are drained, spread out and allowed to sprout for approximately one week. During this period, the grain produces the enzyme amylase, which in turn converts some of the starch in the grain's endosperm into fermentable sugars.

Stage Three. Kilning (Drying and Roasting). Germination must be arrested before the growing sprouts consume too much of their food, the sugar. This is accomplished by slowly heat-drying the malted (germinated) barley in a kiln. For a pale-hued and mild-tasting beer, the brewer removes the malted barley as soon as it is thoroughly dry. For a darker and more flavorful beer, the brewer leaves the barley malt in the kiln and gradually raises its temperature. The longer the malt stays in the kiln, the more it will become roasted and caramelized, and the darker, fuller-flavored and sweeter the brew will be.

Stage Four. Milling. The dried barley malt is sieved to remove the sprouts. It is then ground into grist in a mill machine to facilitate the extraction of sugars and other soluble substances in Stage Five. (Note: Nowadays, Stages One through Four are often performed by a commercial maltster, an outside firm that specializes in malting. The brewery buys the milled barley malt ready for mashing—Stage Five.)

Stage Five. Mashing. The milled barley malt is mixed with hot water in a large vessel called the mashing tun (rhymes with bun). If the brewer uses adjuncts, they are incorporated at this time. (They must be precooked to make their starch soluble.)

Stage Five has two primary goals: to convert more of the starch into sugar and to extract, by infusion, the soluble substances including sugar. The mash, which resembles thin porridge, is subjected to temperatures of approximately 150°F for several hours. It is then filtered, and the sugar-rich liquid becomes known as the wort (rhymes with Bert).

Being frugal, brewers augment the wort by spraying the strained solids of the mash with hot water to extract most of the soluble substances that they may still be harboring. This spraying substage is called sparging. The strained solids are sold as animal fodder.

Stage Six. Boiling. The broad definition of the word "brewing" comprises Stages One through Nine. Technically, it refers only to Stage Six. It begins when the wort is transferred to the kettle (called the copper) and boiled. The flavoring and aromatic hops are added, respectively, at the beginning and end of this process, which generally lasts an hour or two. Afterward, the hops are filtered out and the hot wort is speedily cooled in a specially designed refrigeration unit. The shock of this rapid cooling helps clarify the brew.

Stage Seven. Fermenting. The cooled wort is pitched (mixed) with yeast in a huge fermenting tank. Soon the yeast cells multiply and feed on the sugar, producing alcohol and carbon dioxide. The ale-producing yeast strains gradually rise to the top of the developing brew, helping create a surface foam. In contrast, the lager-producing counterparts slowly sink to the bottom of the vat, producing a sediment.

The fermenting process usually takes eight to twelve days at a temperature between 35° to 49°F for lagers and five to six days at 53° to 69°F for ales. The "green beer" as it is now called, is filtered on its way to the maturation tank.

Few Scotch drinkers realize that, except for the use of hops, the process for making their barley spirit is virtually identical to that for beer up through the first seven stages outlined in this chapter. At this point, the Scotch and beer producers take different tacks. The Scotch makers distill the "green beer" before they mature and bottle their product. Brewers let the beer mature and then bottle it without distilling it.

Stage Eight. Maturing. During this stage, the beer develops new and pleasing odors and flavors and (we hope) eliminates its rough edges. A sensory metamorphosis occurs because the hundreds of distinct compounds in a recently brewed beer chemically interact with one another, for better or worse. Clarifying and conditioning are also Stage Eight goals.

Lagers are matured for anywhere from several days to several months. Inexpensive, run-of-the-mill beers generally opt for the minimum and quality European brews for the maximum period. The lagering (storage) temperature hovers near 32°F.

Ales do not need a lengthy maturation period. Usually a week or two at the comparatively high 40° to 45°F temperature suffices.

Beer is clarified by several means as it rests in the maturation vat. Both gravity and the coldness of the liquid naturally precipitate some of the suspended matter, which sinks to the bottom of the tank, forming a sediment. More stubborn suspended microparticles are usually coagulated with fining agents such as isinglass, carrageen (Irish moss) and silica gel.

The term *conditioning* has a special meaning to a brewer. It means to increase the effervescence of a beer after it has been fermented by inducing a secondary fermentation (distinct from the previous fermentation in Stage Seven). This process, more often than not, takes place in the maturation vat and can be accomplished in one of four basic ways: natural conditioning, krausening, priming and reyeasting.

Natural conditioning automatically happens if the brew still contains live yeast cells and has not been fully fermented in Stage Seven. This is the oldest and most traditional of the various conditioning methods.

Krausening involves adding a small amount of a partially fermented brew to a fully fermented one. The whole batch is enlivened when the unfermented sugars of the young brew ferment.

Priming is the process of adding fermentable sugar such as corn syrup to a fully fermented beer. Live yeast cells devour the newly introduced sugar and produce the sought-after effervescence.

Reyeasting is the fourth method. It entails adding a smidgen of fresh yeast to a brew that contains fermentable sugars but lacks live yeast cells.

Natural conditioning, krausening, priming and reyeasting can also be performed on brew after it has been transferred from the maturation vat to a cask or bottle. The resulting brews are called, respectively, cask-conditioned and bottle-conditioned beers.

A pseudo-type conditioning is carbonic injection. Because this technique saves money, it is popular with many high-tech breweries. Carbon dioxide gas is pumped under high pressure into an airtight maturation vat or other enclosure. Given sufficient pressure, some of the gas is forced into the beer. Soda pop makers employ this method. Carbon dioxide gas for carbonic injection can be acquired by two means. It can be purchased by the brewer as a commodity. Or, the brewer can use some of the carbon dioxide gas captured and stored as it rises off the brew during the fermentation stage.

Stage Nine. Racking, Canning and Bottling. Traditional draft beer is racked; that is, it is transferred directly, with no or minimal filtration, from the maturation vat into sterilized barrels or kegs. The dregs (sediment) stay behind. If the brew is pasteurized, centrifuged or microfiltered in any way, it is not traditional draft beer.

The primary purpose of pasteurization is to extend shelf life by killing beer-spoiling microorganisms. (The process also kills yeast cells, thereby arresting any chance of further fermentation—the beer is no longer alive.) Since bottled beer and canned beers generally have longer and warmer storage lives than barrel or keg beers, there is more of a need to pasteurize those brews.

Bottled and canned beer is normally pasteurized via the tunnel method. The sealed containers are passed through a tunnel-like apparatus and gradually heated with hot water sprays to a temperature of about 140°F, then cooled. The total process takes slightly less than one hour.

Flash pasteurization is an alternative microbiological stabilizing process. The brew is heated to about 185°F for 20 to 30 seconds before being placed in the bottle, can, barrel or keg.

Both the tunnel and flash methods only partially sterilize the brew. Complete sterilization is possible, but would require such high heat that the beer would strongly smack of scorched toffee, a flavor reminiscent of canned evaporated milk. Tunnel and flash pasteurization do enough flavor damage as it is. Between the two methods, flash pasteurization is preferable.

Centrifuging helps clarify a brew by whirling the beverage in a spinning vessel at thousands of G's. The centrifugal force pushes most of the precipitate matter from a brew. A single liquid ounce of freshly fermented beer contains millions of yeast cells, not to mention the untold number of other suspended solids. If a beer is to be brilliantly clear (as the average American beer drinker demands), then it must be "polished" by being passed through microporous filters. This process—microfiltering—takes out most of the suspended matter, including beer-spoiling microorganisms. It simultaneously devastates some of the body, aroma and flavor.

New and Substandard. There is a new brewery method that is no friend to quality. It's called heavy or high-gravity brewing. The beer is brewed in high strength then diluted with water prior to bottling or canning. This technique saves the brewery money because it can increase its output without having to expand its facilities.

THE RESULTING
ALCOHOLIC STRENGTH

We get a "kick" out of beer from the colorless ethyl alcohol, C_2H_2OH. Government agencies in America measure its strength in two basic ways: by weight and by volume. Some states use the "by weight" measurement, others use the "by volume" method. The "by weight" figure is about 20% lower than the "by volume" statistic because alcohol weighs less than an equivalent volume of water. A beer that measures 4.0% by volume has the same alcoholic strength as one that measures 3.2% by weight.

FIGURE 3

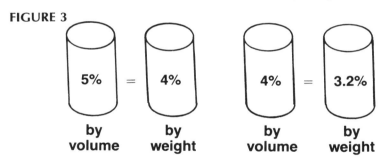

We get a "kick" out of beer from the colorless ethyl alcohol,

Brewers sometimes use the British specific gravity (or density) measurement system. Water is assigned a rating of 1000 and a beer's density is measured relative to that standard. To convert the specific gravity to the approximate equivalent in alcoholic strength by weight, divide the last two digits of that number by thirteen. Thus, a beer with a specific gravity of 1052 would have an alcoholic strength by weight of roughly 4.0%.

Brewers also classify alcoholic strength by degrees Plato (°P), an offshoot of the once popular degrees Balling. It measures the concentration of solids in unfermented brew. You can calculate its rough equivalent nin alcoholic strength by weight by dividing the degree Plato by three. Accordingly, if a beer had a 12°P rating, its alcoholic strength by weight would be about 4.0%.

Though it is true that the better brands of American lager usually are more potent than the ordinary ones, there comes a point of diminishing returns. I would not want a strength of more than 4.0% by weight in a mildly flavored beer because the mouthfeel sensation of the alcohol would overwhelm the other attributes of the brew. Full-flavored brews can better balance the assaulting boldness of abundant alcohol.

High-octane beers are not suited for scorching weather because they can easily raise your body temperature, increasing your discomfort. If one of your goals is to quench your thirst with a couple of bottles of beer, select a less alcoholic brew. American light beers would seem to fit the bill because of their relatively low alcoholic content, but I find more pleasure in a cool glass of water than in these queer beers. The perfect choice is a quality beer of moderate stength—Beck's, Heineken or Kronenbourg, for instance.

Malt beverages with alcoholic strengths of less than 0.5% by weight are classified as near beers by the federal government. Marketers label these brews as "nonalcoholic" or "alcohol-free" beers. Since the alcohol content can be just a shade below 0.5% these terms may be misnomers. That degree of alcohol content may be insignificant to most of us, but not to alcoholics trying to stay on the wagon.

True beers can exceed 10%, but the global average is approximately 4% by weight (5% by volume). By comparison, most table wines fall into the 10 to 14% zone and spirits in the 40 to 50% (80 to 100 proof) range.

In some states, if the alcoholic content of a lager exceeds 5.0% by weight (6.2% by volume), the brewer is prohibited from using the word "lager" or "beer" on the label. Rather, the brewer must use another designation such as malt liquor, ale, stout or porter—even though the brew may be a lager beer.

State laws often set upper limits for the most potent type of beer that can be sold. In Utah, no beer—including malt liquor—can exceed 3.2% alcohol by weight. Thus, the Colt 45 that is shipped to that state has an alcoholic content of only 3.2%. I'm sure that at least a few Utah citizens buy it under the impression that it has the extra kick implicitly promised in the nationally televised commercials.

Based on the latest data compiled by the Beer Institute (formerly the United States Brewers Association), the maximum permissible alcoholic contents for beverages sold in the various states is as follows:

STATE	MAXIMUM PERMISSIBLE ALCOHOLIC CONTENT
Alabama	4% by weight, 5% by volume
Alaska	No limit
Arizona	No limit
Arkansas	5% by weight for most malt beverages
California	4% by weight for beer; no limit for ale, etc.
Colorado	3.2% by weight except for malt liquor
Connecticut	No limit
Delaware	No limit
District of Columbia	No limit
Florida	3.2% in dry counties; no limit elsewhere
Georgia	6% by volume
Hawaii	No limit
Idaho	4% by weight in nonstate stores
Illinois	No limit in most areas
Indiana	No limit
Iowa	5% by weight in nonstate stores
Kansas	3.2% by weight except for liquor store package sales
Kentucky	No limit in most areas
Louisiana	6% by volume in most areas; 3.2% by weight in dry areas
Maine	No limit
Maryland	No limit
Massachusetts	12% by weight
Michigan	No limit
Minnesota	3.2% by weight for most malt beverages
Mississippi	4% by weight
Missouri	3.2% by weight. Exception: 5% for "malt liquor"
Montana	7% by weight
Nebraska	No limit
Nevada	No limit
New Hampshire	6% by volume in nonstate stores
New Jersey	No limit
New Mexico	No limit
New York	No limit
North Carolina	6% by volume
North Dakota	No limit
Ohio	6% by weight
Oklahoma	3.2% by weight except for liquor store package sales
Oregon	4% by weight for beer; 8% by weight for other malt beverages
Pennsylvania	No limit
Rhode Island	No limit

STATE	MAXIMUM PERMISSIBLE ALCOHOLIC CONTENT
South Carolina	5% by weight
South Dakota	3.2% by weight for "low point beer"; 6% by weight for "high point"
Tennessee	5% by weight for most malt beverages
Texas	4% by weight for "beer"; no limit for others
Utah	3.2% by weight in nonstate stores
Vermont	6% by volume in nonstate stores
Virginia	No limit
Washington	8% by weight in nonstate stores and unlicensed establishments
West Virginia	4.2% by weight; 6% by volume
Wisconsin	5% by weight for most malt beverages
Wyoming	No limit

In order to accommodate the differences in state regulations, most national brands are brewed in two strengths, one at 3.2%, the other as high as 5.0% alcohol by weight. Few beer drinkers are aware of this product variation.

In America, the alcoholic content of domestic lagers normally ranges from 3.2 to 4.5% by weight (4.0 to 5.6% by volume). The by-weight percentage is usually in the 2.4 to 3.2 range for light beers, 3.2 to 4.5 for lagers, 3.2 to 5.0 for ales, and 3.2 to 8.0 for malt liquors.

Most imported pale lagers have alcoholic strengths between 3.5 and 4.5% by weight. The ranges are 4.0 to 5.0% for most pale ales and 4.0 to 6.0% for most dark ales and bock beers. Some imports, such as Carling Elephant Malt, are considerably stronger. If you buy brew in a state that has set a low ceiling on alcoholic strength in beer, the above statistics are academic.

Occasionally you see X's on a label as with Mackeson XXX Stout and Dos Equis (which means "two X's" in Spanish). The X's originally denoted quality or the number of times a spirit was distilled, but today they generally signify relative strength as defined by the individual brewer. One XX-rated brand may be more potent than a competitor's XXX product.

Military bases cannot serve potent brews. The maximum limit is 3.2% alcohol by weight.

Canada and some other foreign countries require brewers to list the alcoholic strength on the label. In most states in America, this listing is prohibited by law. In those states that require the listing, the information is usually restricted to wording such as "contains not more than 3.2% alcohol by weight" or "alcoholic content is in excess of 3.2% by weight." The exact alcoholic content is not revealed to the consumer. Only three states currently permit a specific listing and then only when the alcohol exceeds a certain level (4% by weight in Oregon, 5% by weight in Arkansas and 7% by weight in Montana).

Two final notes on alcohol. The folk wisdom that you shouldn't drink too much on an empty stomach is valid. Food in your stomach slows the absorption of the alcohol into your bloodstream. However, the popular notion that you should give a drunk strong black coffee has led to many deaths. Caffeine doesn't sober up intoxicated people, it just turns them into wide-awake drunks.

PART SIX

HOW BEER
IS CLASSIFIED

Beer is classified in many ways. Some beer categories relate to price, season, degree of strength, production processes or geographic origin. Others concern style—the overall characteristics that distinguish one group of beers from all others.

Because there are so few industry-wide categorization standards, terms like light beer have acquired dual meanings. Other groupings such as ale and amber beer overlap. This mini-encyclopedia will help guide you through the linguistic maze.

Ale vs. Lager—Most of the world's major beers are either ales or lagers. The ale group includes:

> Alt
> Barley Wine
> Bitter
> Brown
> Kölsch
> Mild
> Pale Ale
> Porter
> Scotch Ale
> Stout
> Trappist

These brew types are lagers:

> American-style Pale Lager
> Bock
> Bremener-Hamburger
> Dark
> Doppelbock
> Dortmunder
> International-style Pale Lager
> Light Beer (low calorie)
> Light Beer (pale lager)
> Marzenbier
> Munich Dark Beer (*dunkel*)
> Munich Pale Lager (*helles*)
> Pale Lager
> Pilsner/Pilsener

Ales are "top-fermented" and lagers are "bottom-fermented:" this is an important distinction. The yeast strains that produce traditional ales eventually rise to the surface of the beer and those that yield traditional lagers gradually sink to the bottom of the vat during the fermentation process. (See Part 5, "How Beer Is Made.")

The aging processes are dissimilar too. Quality lagers are aged at the brewery for one to three months, sometimes longer. Traditional ales, in contrast, are generally given a shorter aging process. Some of them are either bottle-conditioned (aged in the bottle), or cask-conditioned for a few days in the cool cellar of the pub.

Because of these and other differences, there are sensory distinctions between lagers and ales in general. The typical lager is:

> clearer
> lighter-hued
> more carbonated
> crisper
> drier
> maltier
> less hoppy and aromatic
> lighter-bodied
> lower in alcohol

However, don't be surprised if you can't tell the difference between an ale and lager in a blind tasting because ales and lagers are today produouced in a wide variety of overlapping styles. You can, for instance, drink strong (13%) lagers and weak (3%) ales, considerably hoppy lagers and virtually hopless ales, and brownish black lagers and pale golden ales.

To complicate matters further, many high-tech lager and ale brands are made with recently developed yeast strains that exhibit behavioral traits of both top- and bottom-fermented yeasts. Yet other brands are lagales (qq.v.).

Federal and state laws also hamper identification. In many states a lager with an alcoholic strength of 5% or more cannot be called a lager or beer. Rather than being forced to call their product a malt liquor, a brewery may slap an ale label on its bottom-fermented (lager) product. Sometimes the motive for mis-labeling is greed: the brewery wants to exploit those Americans who "think ale but drink lager."

Alt—Though this is a type of ale, its name has no linguistic con-nection with the word "ale." Germans call this brew alt (meaning "old") to distinguish it from lager, the relatively new style of beer that began to gain popularity in Germany in the nineteenth century. *Alt* is still the major type of beer brewed in the Düsseldorf and Münster areas of West Germany. It has a noticeably hoppy flavor, reasonable maltiness and moderate alcoholic content. The hue is typically reddish brown though a few specimens like Pinkus Alt are honey golden.

Amber Beer—Describes a brew like Bass Ale with a depth of hue halfway between pale and dark. For some products, the terms coppery or brassy are more appropriate.

American-Style Pale Lager—Budweiser and Miller High Life are the two prominent examples of this style, which comprises scores of national and regional brands and accounts for 90% of the domestic beer consumed in this country.

Except for American-style light and low-alcohol beers, this style is the blandest, lightest-bodied and faintest-hued of the various pilsener (q.v.) styles. It is also blatantly carbonated. Scant flavor character emerges because the brewers liberally use adjuncts, such as corn or rice, and excessively pasteurize and/or microfilter their brews. The resulting beverage offends few souls but neither does it excite discerning palates.

There is minimal brand difference. This was not the case several decades ago when even the big brands were distinctive. If you could cross-taste a Pabst Blue Ribbon of yesteryear with one of today, you would swear they were entirely different brands. Budweiser has evolved, too.

Anniversary Beer—Brewed to commemorate a special occasion, such as a brewery's anniversary. Typically, the brewer invests extra time and money into producing this beer—and charges a premium. "Celebration," "Jahrhundred" and "Jubilee" are alternative names. Christmas and Holiday Beers (q.v.) are similar.

Barley Wine—The British call this ale a wine rather than a beer because it has an alcoholic content approaching that of wine. It is a beer, nonetheless, and has a dark brown hue and, usually, a bittersweet flavor.

Berliner Weisse—Because it has a lily-white head and an extremely pale body, this wheat beer (q.v.) became known as *Weissbier*, meaning "white beer." Berliner Weisse is usually made with a 1:3 wheat-to-barley ratio, and is low in alcohol. The brewer infuses the developing beer with a lactic acid (sour milk) culture, which is partially responsiible for the dry, sharp flavor. Berlin bartenders usually proffer it to you in an oversized, bowl-shaped stemmed glass and, to offset the brew's high acidity, lace it with raspberry syrup.

Bière De Garde—From France comes this beer that is traditionally sold in a corked bottle: it is meant to be aged in a cellar as wines are. Nowadays, the product can be top- or bottom-fermented. It is amber-hued, malty, and full-bodied with an above average alcoholic content. Brasseurs Bière de Paris (formerly Lutèce) is the brand you are most likely to see in the United States.

Bitter Ale—This draught brew is usually highly hopped and, thus, called "bitter ale" to distinguish it from "mild ale," another mainstay of England's pubs. The carbonation is low but the head can be generous. In most instances, the palate is dry, the nose aromatic, the hue amber and the alcoholic content moderate. Bitter is made with barley malt, possibly mixed with corn and rice adjuncts. When bottled, bitter ale is called pale ale.

Bremener-Hamburger Pale Lager—Northern West Germany, in and around the cities of Bremen and Hamburg, is the home of this style. Beck's is the best-selling brand. Of the leading pilsener (q.v.) styles, the Bremener-Hamburger lagers are the driest, crispiest and hoppiest of the lot. Malt flavor is relatively limited.

Bock—Some historians say that the word "bock" is an abbreviated corruption of Einbeck, the name of the Hanseatic League town in northern Germany where this style of beer apparently originated. Other experts insist that bock is a derivative of a Germanic word meaning male goat. Take your pick. What is myth, though, is the widely held belief that bock is made from the dregs removed from the vats during spring cleaning. (Casks must be thoroughly scrubbed after each batch throughout the year if the brew is to be palatable.)

Bock, a lager, is closely identified with Munich, where the local brewers now produce it for year-round consumption rather than just for the spring Bockbier Festival. Bockbier can be pale or, more likely, dark brown. Its minimum alcoholic content is about 6%. Doppelbock (q.v.) is the high-octane version.

Typically, a Bockbier is full bodied, has obvious maltiness and hoppiness, and is fairly sweet, sometimes even syrupy. French bocks are untraditionally weak and the equally ersatz American versions tend to be uncomplex and sugary rather than malty sweet.

Brown Ale—Most brown ales are dark hued with copper or ruby tinges, full flavored and medium sweet to sweet. They are, more or less, the bottled equivalents of the mild draft sold in English pubs.

Budget-priced Beer—This is the lowest of the five standard "Price-Based Classifications" (q.v.). These beers are geared for the tens of millions of shoppers for whom cost, rather than taste, is the overriding consideration.

Burton Ale—See PALE ALE.

Celebration Beer—Can be an Anniversary (q.v.) or Holiday (q.v.) beer.

Christmas Beer—Certain European and now New World breweries make a specialty beer for yuletide consumption. These brews are amber to dark hued, richly flavored with a sweetish palate, full-bodied and high in alcohol. Norway's Aass Jule, Mexico's Noche Buena and Our Special Ale from San Francisco's Anchor Brewing Company are three illustrations. "Holiday Beer" is an alternative name.

Cream Ale—Not a true ale since most are lagales (q.v.). A cream ale is characteristically sweet but otherwise bland because of scant hop and malt flavors. Gassiness is another shortcoming.

Dark Lager—Compared to pale lagers (q.v.), dark lagers are usually richer, maltier, sweeter, fuller bodied, more aromatic and, of course, considerably deeper hued. Traditional dark lagers, including the celebrated Munich *dunkel Biers* (literally, "dark beers"), are colored and flavored with unadulterated roasted barley grain or malt. To cut costs, the brewers of the new-fangled dark lagers often accomplish this same mission by adding non-maltose caramel or roasted barley malt extract. This method cuts costs but gives the brew a disagreeable caramel candy flavor.

Dessert Brew—Style includes richly sweet brews. Gouden Carolus from Belgium is an example.

Diet Beer—In some parts of the world, the sobriquet "diet beer" defines a low-sugar or -carbohydrate (but not necessarily a low-calorie) brew designed for diabetics. In America, the term is usually used to describe any low-calorie beer irrespective of other attributes.

Domestic Beer—See IMPORTED VS. DOMESTIC BEER.

Doppelbock—"Double bock," as the German term translates, is stronger than regular *Bockbier* (q.v.). Its alcoholic content ranges from nearly 8% to slightly over 13% by volume. Its flavor is decidedly malty. You can usually spot a Bavarian Doppelbock by its name. Chances are it will end with an "ator" suffix, like Kulminator.

Dortmunder—This pale lager style is brewed in the northern German city of Dortmund. It is hoppier than the Munich style to the south but less so than the Bremener-Hamburger (q.v.) style to the far north. At the same time, it is less malty than the Munich style but more so than the Bremener-Hamburger style. Compared to Pilsner Urquell (q.v.), the Dortmunder style (Dortmunder Kronen Classic, for example) has a deeper blond hue and a less pronounced hoppy palate. Dortmunders have characteristically flowery aromas.

When you see the word "export" (q.v.) on the label of a Dort-munder beer, you can almost certainly deduce that the alcoholic content of the brew is above average. Dortmunders labeled simply as "Pilsener" are generally not as strong.

Draft (Draught) Beer—In the tightest sense of the term, a draft beer is one that is naturally carbonated, unpasteurized, minimally filtered and drawn by the server directly from a wooden barrel. These beers are rare in America. A broader, nontraditional definition includes any brew tapped by the server directly from a wooden barrel or metal keg, regardless of whether it has been pasteurized, ultra-filtered or artificially carbonated. When a state-side bartender says "draft beer," this is the type he usually has in mind. There is a third and brazenly misleading usage of the term draft beer. I'm referring to bottled "draft beer." Though these mislabeled products are unpasteurized, they lack the rich flavor of real draft beer because they are hyperfiltered. The difference between draft, bottled and canned beer is further discussed in Part One, "Buying, Storing and Serving Tips."

Dunkel—See DARK LAGER.

Export Beer—In Germany, and especially in the city of Dor-tmund, the appellation "export beer" describes a smooth, rela-tively full-bodied brew that has been purposely imbued with a higher than usual alcoholic content in order to enhance its shippability.

Another and more general definition of export beer is any brew that is sold abroad. These beers are sometimes custom brewed for foreign taste preferences and, consequently, are not identical to the same brand of beer drunk by the citizens in the country of origin.

I've also seen the word "export" boldly printed on the labels of beers that are largely or totally consumed in their country of ori-gin. The Claussen Export beer of Colombia is an example. Many of these brews use the term "export" because it has cachet and implies superior quality.

Generic Beer—If a beer is sold without a brand name, it is called a generic beer. Sometimes the only conspicuous word on the label is "beer." Generic brands are budget-priced brews (q.v.).

Hefe-Weizen Beer—See WHEAT BEER.

Holiday Beer—Brewed especially for the Yuletide (see CHRISTMAS BEER) or a local festival, in which case it could also be called a Celebration Beer.

Helles—See MUNICH PALE LAGER.

Homemade Brew—This term is self-explanatory. See the chapter on "Home Brewing" in Part Seven, "A Barrel of Miscellanea" starting on page 242.

House Brand Beer—See PRIVATE LABEL BEER.

Ice Beer—The brewer is able to give his product a remarkably heady status (more than 13% alcohol) by cooling his brew to a temperature below the freezing point of water (32°F) but above that of alcohol (-173°F). When he removes and discards some of the formed ice, the brew ends up with a higher alcohol-to-water ratio.

Imported vs. Domestic Beer—The denotation of these terms is obvious. Their connotations are another matter. "Imported" beer has a better image than "domestic" beer beause the *average* imported brand in the U.S. is superior in quality to the *average* domestic beer. Only an American chauvinist would deny this unfortunate fact of life. Specifically, the average imported brew when compared to its domestic counterpart will likely have more character. Chances are it will be hoppier, fuller bodied, more distinctly flavored, less carbonated, aged longer and made with fewer adjuncts and additives, if any at all. It will also tend to be more alcoholic and costly.

Indian Pale Ale (IPA)—See PALE ALE.

International-Style Pale Lager—Carlsberg (Denmark), Carta Blanca (Mexico), Heineken (Netherlands), Kirin (Japan), Kronenbourg (France), Molson Canadian, and San Miguel (Philippines) are but seven examples of this widely produced style. Even some German and English breweries are now making international-style pale lagers, both for home and foreign consumption.

I've tasted numerous international-style pale lagers around the globe and have come to realize that their quality and characteristics vary thunderously from country to country, brand to brand. The Canadian brands, for instance, tend to be on the sweet side while those in Scandinavia are usually dry.

Few international-style pale lagers are more than medium-bodied or exceed a 5% alcoholic strength. A growing number of specimens, including the Tsing Tao from China, are noticeably thin. International-style pale lagers, on average, are more flavorful than the American-style pale lagers (q.v.) but less so than, say, a Pilsner Urquell (q.v.). The best offerings have an elegant nose and palate, making them ideal partners for subtly flavored dishes.

Jahrhundred—See ANNIVERSARY BEER.

Jubilee—See ANNIVERSARY BEER.

Kölsch—A West German ale brewed in the Bonn-Cologne metropolis (the brew derives its name from latter city). Kölsch has a very pale brassy gold hue, a mild malt flavor with some lactic tartness, moderate alcoholic content and a tame carbonation.

Lagales—Brewers concoct these hybrid brews by blending bottom-fermented lagers with top-fermented ales.

Lager—See ALE VS. LAGER.

Lambic Beer—The wheat beer called lambic is produced only within marching distance of Brussels, Belgium. It is one of the world's distinctive beers: the brewers don't have to add yeast to their vats since their brew is spontaneously fermented by the beneficial strains of airborne wild yeast natural to the area. As any of hundreds of different wild yeast strains may be the one to ferment the malt solution, the characteristics of any given lambic brand may vary from batch to batch.

The basic lambic is a reasonably full-bodied beverage with an acidic, yeasty palate. It can be drunk young or, preferably, after it has been aged for up to a year or two in wooden casks. A sweet, reddish variant with a medium-to-high alcoholic strength is kriek, a lambic that undergoes a secondary fermentation when the brewer adds black cherries to the vat. Framboise lambic is similar, but rasberries are used. Another offshoot is the gueuze-lambic, a blend of different types of lambic. It is twice fermented and aged, and has a dry, fruity, champagnelike effervescence. Yet another subtype is the sugar-primed faro-lambic. It is typically weaker in body and strength than the other basic lambic styles.

Light Beer vs. Light Beer—"Light" on a label may not mean what you think it means because there are two types of light beer. While both are pale hued, one is a low-calorie and the other a regular-calorie pale lager (q.v.).

The American brands use the term light beer for their low-calorie products. Most European brands use the term light beer to distinguish their pale lagers from their dark-hued lagers (q.v.). When you see "light" on the Beck's bottle, for instance, it refers to the lightness of hue rather than the calorie count.

I suspect that most of the people who drink American-style light beers have not seen the light. These brews are scarcely more than bland, watered down beers. To add insult to injury, brewers usually charge the same for them as they do for their more flavorful regular brews, yet American-style light beers are less expensive to produce because they contain fewer nonwater ingredients, including cereal grains. The customer is also being shortchanged because the alcoholic content of these products is typically about 20% less than for regular beer.

Suggested Experiment

Mix one part water with two parts regular beer. Compare the flavor, body and per-glass cost of this concoction with those of a light beer of the same brand.

When low calorie/carbohydrate light beer first hit the market, few men—the people who consume virtually all of the beer produced—purchased it. To cut down on calories wasn't perceived as "manly." Then, a clever marketer came up with the idea of advertising "less filling" rather than "less fattening." Instead of emphasizing the beer's dietary virtues, he stressed the fact that the average drinker could consume more "light" than normal beer. Since being able to drink vast amounts of beer is often considered "manly" in beer drinking circles, the sales of light beers sky-rocketed.

Granted, American-style light beers do have fewer calories, and calories are certainly an important consideration to anyone like me who has to watch his waistline. But the relatively small amount of calories you save hardly justifies the lost pleasure.

Low Alcohol Beer—This brew has less than 2% alcohol content by weight (2.4% by volume). This is approximately half the strength of regular American beers. Low alcohol beers have noticeably weak flavors and bodies.

Low Calorie Beer—See LIGHT BEER VS. LIGHT BEER.

Luxury-priced Beer—This is the highest of the five standard "Price-Based Classifications" (q.v.). It embraces most of the imported brands and a growing number of domestic ones such as Anchor Steam Beer. The term "luxury" is relative since the difference in retail price between a luxury-priced beer and a super premium brew is usually only a quarter or two per bottle, a pittance when compared to the corresponding price differential in the wine field.

Malt Beverage—In the most comprehensive sense, a malt beverage is any alcoholic or nonalcoholic drink made with malted (germinated) barley or other grain. In the restricted definition, a malt beverage is a non- or minimally alcoholic malt drink such as near beer (q.v.).

Malt Liquor—Nearly all the malt liquors sold in this country are lagers or lagales (q.v.) that are too alcoholic to be legally labeled lagers or beers. (The reason for this nomenclature policy is discussed in "The Resulting Alcoholic Strength" chapter in Part Five, "How Beer Is Made" starting on page 209.) There are many varieties of malt liquor. The beverage may be pale or dark-hued, sweet or dry, hoppy or not. Colt 45, Schlitz Malt Liquor (the "bull"), and some of the other brands of this style, do a land-office business, but not because of their quality, which they generally lack. The prime reason why so many people drink them is their wallop. Malt liquors usually give the customer more alcohol per dollar than do wines, spirits and regular beers. To put it bluntly, most malt liquors imbibers want a relatively cheap high—and beer advertisers are more than aware of this motivation. A malt liquor, by the way, is not a true liquor, a term reserved for beverages like vodka and whiskey that are distilled after they have been fermented.

Marzenbier—Vienna style, as this style is also known, is an amber lager with an energetic malty flavor, timid hoppy palate and a moderately strong alcoholic strength. Dos Equis (XX) from Mexico comes close to fitting that description.

Marzenbier means "March beer" in German. It is traditionally brewed in Munich during March, aged and stored in cool caves through the hot summer months, and quaffed in the fall, especially during the Oktoberfest season.

Mild Ale—Along with bitter ale and stout (qq.v.), this style is a mainstay of the British pub, especially in England north of London. Most mild ales are draft-served, dark-hued, mildly-hopped, well-malted and pointedly sweet. Alcoholic content is moderate.

Milk Stout—See SWEET STOUT.

Modified European Beers—Some American firms purchase the domestic licensing rights to use the name of a world famous European brew, such as Löwenbräu or Tuborg, on beer they make in the United States. Unfortunately, the American producer imports the name, not the quality, because the U.S. product is made with chemical preservatives and less expensive ingredients. It also undergoes a different brewing process and is aged for a shorter period.

Another breed of modified European beers are those like Steinhäuser that are brewed, but not consumed, in their homeland because they were created specifically for export in the hope of pleasing the perceived American taste. Related to that genre of beers are American-brewed beverages, like Erlanger, which are packaged and advertised, in part, to give the impression that there is an identical product being consumed in Europe.

Munich Dark Beer (*dunkel*)—See DARK LAGER.

Munich Pale Lager (*helles*)—The Bavarian city of Munich in southern West Germany is the home of this popular beverage fashioned by such illustrious brewers as Augustiner, Hacker-Pschorr, Hofbräuhaus, Löwenbräu (which does not brew the American Löwenbräu, a lesser product), Paulaner and Spaten. Local cities call it *helles Bier* ("light beer" in German), refering to the brew's depth of color. The salient difference between this style and the various pilseners (q.v.), also pale lagers, is in the proportion of the ingredients. Munich pale lagers are heavily malted, lightly hopped. The opposite is true for pilseners (except for the American-style which is both tamely hopped and malted). The Munich pale lager is usually slightly less alcoholic than the non-American pisener products.

Near Beer—Alcohol-free, nonalcohol and de-alcoholized beer are other popular names for this brew. These alternative names are misleading because virtually all near beers have an alcoholic content of somewhere between 0.1 and 0.4% alcohol by weight. (In the U.S., a brew is legally classified as a near beer if its alcoholic content is less than 0.5%)

Brewers use various methods to keep the alcoholic content below the limit. Some brew the beer in the normal manner, then extract the unwanted alcohol by vacuum distillation. Others use a special yeast that only partially ferments the beverage.

Near beers are not true beers and, accordingly, are not rated in this book.

Non-alcoholic Beer—See NEAR BEER.

Oktoberfest—A dark (*dunkel*) beer that was originally brewed for Munich's annual Oktoberfest. Nowadays, the beer is also brewed for year round consumption but this variety usually has less alcohol than the type made specifically for Munich's famous rites of fall.

Pale Ale—This sobriquet describes a bottled bitter ale (q.v.). As with the word bitter, pale is used as a comparative term. Though the brew is amber, it's called pale to emphasize how light it is versus the blackish stouts and porters. Pale ale is also known as Burton (because it originated in the English town of Burton on Trent) and IPA or Indian Pale Ale (because it was brewed for shipment to India).

Pale Lager—This is an umbrella descriptive for a broad range of clear, crisp, dry, light golden-hued lagers. Most fall into one of these six basic classifications:

> American style (a pilsener)
> Bremener-Hamburger style (a pilsener)
> Dortmunder style (a pilsener)
> International style (a pilsener)
> Munich style (*helles*)
> Pilsner (the original pilsener)

Each is defined under its own heading. In addition, there is a special pale lager category called American-style light beer which is discussed in the "Light Beer vs. Light Beer" entry on page 224.

Pilsner/Pilsener—The archetypal pilsner is brewed in the Bohemian town of Plzen in Czechoslovakia. The Western European appellation for this world celebrated beer is Pilsner Urquell, the German translation of Plzensky Prazdroj. Urquell (Prazdroj) means "fountainhead" or, more broadly, "the original source." The pale lager Pilsner Urquell is uniformly excellent.

In addition to the proprietary pilsner product (spelled with only one e), there are generic pilseners (spelled with two e's or simply abbreviated to "pils"), brewed approximately in the style of the Czech original. These pilseners vary in quality from excellent to mediocre and usually fit within one of these pale lager styles: American, Bremener-Hamburger, Dortmunder and International (qq.v.).

Pilsner and pilsener brews are characteristically pale golden-hued and effervescent with a dry, crisp and moderately malted flavor. The Bremener-Hamburger versions are decidedly hoppy. Pilsner Urquell is slightly less so. Dortmunders have a medium-to-bold degree of hoppiness. International-style pilseners are mildly to moderately hoppy, while the American renditions are meekly hopped.

Popular-priced Beer—This is the second lowest of five standard "Price-Based Classifications" (q.v.). They usually retail for a shade less than the premium brands. Nearly all of them are regional brands.

Porter—Supposedly, this ale got its name because eighteenth-century London porters quaffed it by the pitcherful. The popularity of this hybrid brew (originally a blend of ale and two other beers) declined by the middle nineteenth century, though it is now making a limited comeback. Today's porter is typically dark, full-bodied, moderately hopped and medium to medium-high in alcoholic strength. The barley (or barley-malt) is well roasted, giving the brew a characteristic chocolaty, bittersweet flavor.

Premium Beer—Of the five standard "Price-Based Classifications" (q.v.), this is the middle rung. In terms of volume, most of the beer consumed in this country falls within this bracket. Specific brands include Budweiser, Miller High Life, Coor's and Schlitz. The term "premium" is also used by a few unscrupulous, or conceited, brewers for their mundane, mediocre brands. Since there is no official government or industry-wide price or quality standard for "premium," these products can get away with this ruse designed to deceive gullible shoppers.

Price-based Classifications—Beers may be classified into five price-based strata. In descending order of retail cost, they are:

> Luxury priced
> Super Premium
> Premium
> Popular priced
> Budget priced

Each is discussed in its own entry. Keep in mind that while there are quality implications for these categories, there is not necessarily a correlation between a beer's price-based classification and its quality.

Private-label (House Brand) Beer—Some large-scale retailers market their own brand of beer. Generally, these products can be sold at a comparatively low price because the quality is seldom high and the retailer has probably negotiated a sweet deal with a nearby brewery saddled with excess plant capacity. Independent distributors play this game, too. Billy Carter, the ex-president's brother, did not buy a brewery to make the now defunct Billy Beer. Instead, he arranged for a number of established breweries around the country to produce Billy Beer for his firm.

Rauchbier (Smoked Beer)—The beer has a smoky flavor because the malt is dried over a fire of moist beechwood. Rauchbier, a dark lager, is a specialty of the northern Bavarian city of Bamberg.

Russian Imperial Stout—This ale is an aged and rather heavy variant of stout (q.v.) that was originally custom-brewed by the English for shipment via the mercurial Baltic Sea to Catherine the Great and her court in Saint Petersburg. To some extent, it was able to survive this beer-killing voyage because, by design, it was still undergoing fermentation and was generously imbued with alcohol, bitter hops and residual sugar.

Sake—Though most people think of sake as some type of wine or spirit, it is technically a beer because it is brewed rather than vinted or distilled. This popular Japanese beverage differs from regular beers in several ways: Sake is virtually colorless, lacks carbonation, has a relatively potent 14 to 16% alcoholic content and is customarily served at a temperature slightly above 100°F.

Scotch Ale—The term is used on the European continent (primarily in Belgium) to describe a strong ale, dark in hue and bittersweet in flavor. In Scotland the pub expression for this brew is a "wee heavy," though the product is lighter in body and alcoholic strength than the Continental version.

Smoked Beer—See *RAUCHBIER.*

Sparkling Ale—An ale (or pseudo-ale) with a high degree of effervescence and, with few exceptions, a low level of quality. Champale is America's best-selling brand.

Specialty Beer—Beer marketers use this appellation for beers custom-brewed for special audiences or events. Lambic and Christmas beers (qq.v.) are two illustrations.

Steam Beer—San Francisco and steam beer are now synonymous in the beer-drinker's manual. Steam beer is a sort of crossbreed brew, being fermented with lager yeast but at the higher ale fermentation temperature. This method became almost a necessity in the Bay City during the Gold Rush days when ice was scarce or priced sky high. San Franciscans have told me that the name originated because the kegs, when tapped, emitted a piercing hissing sound reminiscent of old-fashioned locomotives. Steam beer is unpasteurized. Its head is expansive, its hue amber and its flavor hoppy. The name is now a registered tradename of the Anchor Brewing Company.

Stout—Once porter (q.v.) became popular, it didn't take long for some British Isle brewers to start fashioning a stout porter, one that was darker, richer, fuller-bodied, maltier, hoppier and more alcoholic and bitter than regular porter. Soon this new style of ale, which is traditionally colored and flavored with well-roasted unmalted barley, became known simply as stout. Dry or Irish-style stout (including Guinness) is the best known stout subtype. Other variations are the sweet stout (q.v.), the heady Russian Imperial Stout (q.v.) and the Samuel Smith Oatmeal Stout, all English. The most unusual stout I have tasted was on the Isle of Man; the brew was enriched with oyster extract.

Strong Ales—This brew is strong in hue, flavor and alcohol. Barley wine and Scotch ale (qq.v.) are well known varieties.

Super Premium Beer—This is the second highest of the five standard "Price-Based Classifications" (q.v.). Michelob and the Miller-brewed Löwenbräu are examples.

Sweet Stout—This style is also known as milk stout because some brewers use lactose (milk sugar) as an ingredient. Compared to dry or Irish-style stouts such as Guinness, the sweet or English-style stouts like Mackeson are decidedly sweet and have low alcoholic contents.

Trappist—Other names for this ale style are abbey and monastery. These ales are brewed in Belgium (the best overall source), Holland, Austria and West Germany. I have sampled many versions, but most can be categorized as being high quality, deep hued and relatively high in alcohol. Some undergo multiple fermentations—first in the fermentation vat, then in the storage cask and finally in the bottle. These usually benefit from one or more years of aging in the bottle. You can expect them to be cloudy.

Vienna Style—See *MARZENBIER*.

Weissbier—The archetype *Weissbier* ("white beer") is Berliner Weisse (q.v.) from Berlin. *Weissbiers* that are made in cities like Munich drop the "Berliner" prefix and are usually darker hued.

Weizenbier—"Wheat beer" (q.v.) is the literal translation of this Bavarian specialty. Compared to Berliner Weisse, the other major wheat beer, Weizenbier has a higher alcoholic content (5% or more by volume) and a greater wheat-to-barley ratio (as high as 2 to 1). It is also fuller-bodied and somewhat fuller-flavored, though not quite as acidy. It is customarily served in a large glass shaped like the lower half of a chubby baseball bat. Customarily, bartenders garnish the beer with a lemon slice.

Wheat Beer—There are two main styles. Berliner Weisse (q.v.) from northern Germany and Weizenbier (q.v.) from southern Germany. Both are top-fermented, noticeably acidy and malty, tamely hopped, made from a combination of wheat and barley malts, and at their peak of popularity during the summer. The high protein content of the wheat helps give these beers a gargantuan head. A wheat beer is often given a dosage of yeast after it is bottled to induce a secondary fermentation which, ultimately, creates sediment, cloudiness, added effervescence and a yeasty nose and flavor. These bottle-conditioned products are sometimes labeled *hefe-weizen* (yeast-wheat).

PART SEVEN

A BARREL OF MISCELLANEA

BEER AND HEALTH

I've heard of many health-related myths about beer. Let's set the record straight.

Myth: Beer is very fattening. The average 12-ounce bottle of regular beer has about 150 calories, the same as an equivalent-size container of Coca-Cola, one normal martini, or one and a half standard 4-ounce servings of dry wine. (American light beer has approximately one-third fewer calories than regular beers.) No one has to convince me that beer is not fattening because I tasted thousands of bottles of beer to research this book and never gained a pound.

Myth: Beer give you a pot belly. Have you ever wondered why some otherwise slim men get pot bellies? It's not because beer is so fattening or because these men have blubber-prone midsections. The most likely answer, I surmised through interviews at bars, is that pot-bellied males often drink the equivalent of a six-pack of beer in one sitting. That puts more than one-half gallon of liquid in the stomach at one time, enough to stretch the stomach muscles excessively. If someone does this often enough, whether with beer or water, the distortion will become permanent.

Myth: Beer is the best thirst quencher. Water is a better choice than beer if your goal is to quench your thirst speedily after, say, three sets of tennis. Beer may be more satisfying psychologically, but your body absorbs water quicker because it has fewer suspended solids.

Myth: Beer ruins your appetite. Quality beer in moderation whets your appetite and promotes digestion by pleasantly stimulating the sensory receptors in your mouth and nasal chamber.

235

Once your brain receives this information, it transmits a signal to your digestive system to start the gastric juices flowing. This is particularly true when the brew is agreeably hopped.

Myth: Beer has scant nutritional value. Though beer is not a highly nutritious food, it is not empty calories either, as are sodas. Beer contributes to your diet some carbohydrates, protein, minerals and B-complex vitamins, including riboflavin and niacin. (American light beers supply the least, and the thick, native village brews of Africa the most, nutrients.)

Myth: Beer is a natural product. Some quality brews, including Anchor Steam Beer and many of the better imported German brands, deserve the descriptive term "natural" because they are made exclusively with cereal grain, hops, water and yeast. Most modern beers, however, are infused with additives. Brewers use them for numerous functions including coloring and flavoring the beer, clarifying the liquid, improving and stabilizing the head, and extending shelf life by hindering oxidation and microbial attack. The danger of indiscriminately adding chemicals was illustrated in Canada in the mid-1960s when dozens of moderately heavy beer drinkers died from drinking beer containing cobalt sulfate. Brewers were just beginning to use this chemical as a head enhancer.

Myth: Beer is not for health-conscious individuals. Despite the use of additives by some brewers, beers—especially the quality brands—can foster and protect good health. German doctors for centuries have been prescribing beer to nursing mothers (it helps their milk flow by relaxing them and it replenishes fluids) and as a general remedy for insomnia and tension. A recent survey of 17,000 Canadians revealed that beer drinkers are sick less often and miss fewer days of work than non-beer drinkers. According to U.S. medical studies, individuals who drink one or two bottles of beer a day have fewer heart attacks than do teetotalers. Brewers have eliminated the carinogenic problem of the mid-1970s by significantly reducing the nitrosamines that are created in the malting process. Finally, as seasoned travelers know, beer is safer than the local drinking water in most areas of the world.

BEER-FOOD AFFINITIES

Did you know that beer goes with a greater variety of foods than wine? It is a perfect companion for the spicy-hot dishes of Mexico, India, Thailand and the Sichuan province of China. Wine is not. I have yet to taste in my travels a single ethnic cuisine—even a mild one such as Cantonese—that is incompatible with beer.

Most Americans wouldn't dream of ordering beer in a fancy French restaurant even though I always spot a few bottles of beer on the table when I dine in the haute cuisine temples of Paris. Thankfully, this American blindspot is gradually disappearing, and I'm seeing more and more sophisticated diners occasionally ordering quality brands of beer in the most exclusive French establishments in New York, including Lutèce, Le Cygne and La Côte Basque. Make no mistake, beer could never supplant wine as the consummate accompaniment to classic French cuisine, but it does offer broad-minded gourmets a pleasant change of pace.

Since most beers go reasonably well with most foods, there is no crucial need for you to concern yourself with learning about specific beer-food couplings unless you happen to be an epicure. If you are, here are a few pointers.

Highly alcoholic brews like Carlsberg Elephant Malt are perfect mates for those chili-hot preparations that make you reach for the nearest fire extinguisher. The more potent the brew, the quicker the pain on your tongue will subside. This occurs because the capsicin compounds in the chili that burn your tongue are soluble in alcohol but not in water. Thus, the increased concentration of alcohol will more speedily wash away the scorching molecules. By the same token, even a minimally alcoholic brew is more effective than a glass of water.

Full-bodied, deep-flavored brews on the order of Guinness Stout pair nicely with hearty peasant stews. Though these beers are too assertive for delicate shellfish, there is a classic exception:

Guinness and oysters, a marriage that was made in heaven.

Dark and amber beers of the German persuasion complement sausages, cold cuts and smoked pork specialties. Weisswurst and Munich Oktoberfest beer is one of my all time favorite duets.

Well-hopped beers, Pilsner Urquell included, go admirably with fat-rich items like roast duck and barbecued spare ribs because the tangy bitterness of the hops helps cut through the fatty taste. These brews also bring out the best in steaks, hamburgers, pizzas and southern fried chicken.

Beers of elegance, like Diekirch Pilsener, are wise choices for subtly seasoned creations from the classic French and Northern Italian cuisines. These brews also harmonize with simply prepared shellfish like boiled lobster.

I am always amazed at the number of natural regional match-ups I encounter on my journeys. Kirin and sushi, San Miguel and adobo, and Gösser and Wienerschnitzel are three illustrations. Many geographic links, though, have disappointed me mainly because of the mediocrity of the local brew.

Don't count too heavily on American-style pale lagers and especially, American light beers to enhance food. These brews are too bland, even for the ballpark hot dog.

Exceptionally sweet beers, like Mackeson Stout, are best savored by themselves unless you are in arm's reach of those traditional salty beer snacks, pretzels and peanuts. (Salt and sugar lower each other's flavor intensity.) To serve a sweet beer with nearly any type of dish would be an injustice to both the potable and the edible. Remember this rule: the less sweet the food, the drier the brew should be.

Beer with Other Beverages

Classic mixed drinks include the Black Velvet (Guinness Stout with champagne) and the Shandy (beer with the nonalcoholic ginger beer or—less traditionally—with lemonade or Seven Up). Pub-crawling Britishers ask for Arf 'n Arf (equal parts of two brews such as mild and bitter) while saloon-sitting Americans call for the boilermaker (a shot of whiskey chased with a glass of beer). Perhaps the most interesting concoction of all is the boilermaker variant that is aptly named the Depth Charge. You drop a shot of spirits into your brew, shot glass and all.

COOKING WITH BEER

Don't pour your next half-empty bottle of beer down the drain. Save it for cooking, as I do. The brew will become flat, but that is of no culinary concern. As a cook you need the beer's flavor and acid, not its effervescence.

The leftover beer must be fresh. Any brew that has sat in an opened bottle on the table at room temperature for more than an hour has probably oxidized and been attacked by airborne acetic bacteria. As soon as you realize that you are not going to finish a brew, promptly cap and refrigerate it. Thus stored, it will remain in usable condition for at least a week. The higher the brew's alcoholic or sugar content, the longer it will keep.

Of course, you don't need leftover beer. A bottle opened expressly for cooking will also do. Whatever your choice, be sure it is a quality product. If you use an ordinary brew in the pot, you will likely end up with an ordinary dish.

The best all-around cooking beers are full-flavored, not too sweet, and high in acid. The last quality—acidity—is essential for marinating, and wheat brews are especially suited for this function. Except for delicately flavored preparations, a dark beer is generally better for cooking than a light-hued one. In all cases, however, I would rather cook with a highly rated pale brew than with a run-of-the-mill dark beer.

If you have children, do not worry about the alcoholic content of beer. The alcohol, which has a lower boiling point than water, should evaporate during the cooking process.

You can normally incorporate refrigerator-cold beer directly into your recipe. For some preparations, like dough, though, you need to bring the refrigerated brew to room temperature beforehand.

The classic beer-infused dish is *Carbonnade Flamande*, Belgian beef stew. (You will find my favorite recipe for it, the one I learned on a small farm in the Bruges countryside, in my *Great Peasant Dishes of the World* cookbook published by Houghton Mifflin.)

Another famous preparation that I've encountered in my travels is Welsh Rabbit: toast, topped with melted cheese, mustard and beer mixture, lightly browned under a grill. In America it is usually called by the less authentic name, Welsh Rarebit.

Any creative cook can adapt a wide variety of recipes to beer cookery by substituting beer for all or part of the water, wine or stock called for in the original recipe. Beer is a splendid cooking ingredient for making baked beans, batter for deep-fried foods (including shrimp), bread, chili con carne, pancakes, poultry stuffing, sauces, soups, stews and waffles.

You can also use beer to braise pork or lamb, poach chicken or seafood, simmer ham or sausages, steam clams or mussels, baste roasts or barbecue shish kebab. Have you ever tried steam-cooking rice in beer? Boiling pasta—or potatoes for potato salad—in beer? Adding 1 teaspoon of beer per egg for omelettes? The possibilities are endless.

To get you started on beer cookery, here's a recipe—*Marinated Beer Chops*—that I created for a new beer cookbook that I have been writing and kitchen testing for the past several years. Someday I hope to finish this volume so that I can share with you the enjoyment of beer cookery.

MARINATED BEER CHOPS
(yield: 4 servings)

4 1-inch-thick pork loin chops
1 cup beer
2 tablespoons unsalted butter
1/2 cup thinly sliced white onions
1/2 teaspoon thyme
1 medium-size bay leaf
1/2 teaspoon lemon juice
1/4 rounded teaspoon salt (or to taste)
1/8 teaspoon ground black peppercorns
4 thickly sliced medium-size mushrooms
2 tablespoons minced red sweet pepper
1 teaspoon chopped parsley

1. Trim the exterior fat off the chops. Marinate the chops in the beer in a covered glass or stainless steel container overnight in the refrigerator. Use fresh or leftover beer, but be sure it's a quality beer.

2. Turn the chops in the morning.

3. Bring the chops and marinade to room temperature. (Remove the container from the refrigerator and let it stand uncovered for one hour before starting Step Four.)

4. Melt the butter over modoerate heat in a large, thick-bottomed sauté pan or skillet. Pat the chops dry with paper toweling. Lightly brown them on both sides in the butter. Transfer the chops to a warm platter and loosely cover them with aluminum foil.

5. Sauté the onions in the pan for one minute, stirring frequently.

6. Add half of the marinade to the pan. Stir in the thyme, bay leaf, lemon juice, salt, black pepper and mushrooms. Bring the mixture to a simmer.

7. Add the chops, coating them on both sides with the sauce. Reduce the heat to low. Cover and cook the chops for 15 minutes without once lifting the lid; if you do, some of the needed cooking steam will escape, Be sure your heat is low. (Use a heat diffuser if necessary.) If the liquid boils rather than gently simmers in Step Seven or Eight, or if the one-inch-thick chops cook for a longer period than called for, the chops will toughen.

8. Discard the bay leaf. Stir in the sweet pepper. Turn the chops. Cover the pan and continue to cook the preparation over low heat for 5 minutes, without lifting the lid.

9. Place the chops on a warm serving platter or individual plates. With the aid of a slotted spoon, smother the chops with the solids in the sauce. (Serve the remaining sauce on the side.) Sprinkle the parsley over the chops. Serve immediately. Enjoy.

HOME BREWING

Prior to the enactment of Public Law 95-458 on February 1, 1979, it was illegal to make beer at home. Millions of Americans did, of course, and I don't know anyone—including me—who was arrested and jailed for the offense.

Today, any adult may legally brew up to 100 gallons of beer per calendar year for personal or family use without having to get a license or pay a tax. If two or more adults live under the same roof, the household limit is 200 gallons. That's 88 cases of beer!

Some of the home brews I've tasted were made by competent amateurs who concocted beverages that were definitely superior to many of the commercial brands. On the other side of the coin, I've sampled home brews (including my efforts) that were better fit for stray alley cats than discriminating palates. At its best, home brew is divine. At its worst, it's ghastly.

There are several advantages to home brewing. It is an exciting hobby, one that can fill you with satisfaction when you drink your own handcrafted product. The better your brew, the more pleasure you will derive. Home brewing can also save you money.

Perhaps you will want to try your hand at home brewing. I won't even attempt to give you instructions because it would require at least a small volume to explain the many intricacies and pitfalls of the process adequately. Fortunately, a number of how-to books on home brewing exist. (See the Bibliography.)

You will need equipment and ingredients. A starter kit can be purchased for as little as $50 from one of the many brewery or winery equipment and supply stores. (Consult your *Yellow Pages*.) Most of the shopowners will be more than willing to give you friendly guidance to help smooth your way through your first several batches.

I strongly recommend that you join the American Home Brewers Association and receive its advice-filled *Zymurgy* magazine. This nonprofit organization also holds an annual conference where members exchange greetings and brewing secrets. Some bring their best efforts to be judged by a panel of experts. For more details about AHBA, write to The American Home Brewers Association, P.O. Box 287, Boulder, Colorado 80306.

COLLECTING

Breweriana, the hobby of collecting beer-related items, is becoming one of America's favorite pastimes. Though it already has hundreds of thousands of devotees, the number will likely double in the next five years.

Collectibles include bottle labels, cans, mugs and steins, beer-theme postcards and postage stamps, plus these brewery advertising and promotional vehicles: ash trays, bottle and can openers, calendars, coasters (one Austrian has nearly 100,000 different specimens), drivers' caps, posters, glasses, lithographed metal trays, signs and tap knobs. The collectors come from all walks of life—blue collar workers, executives, students, professors, priests and more.

Beer cans are by far the leading breweriana specialty, and it's easy to catch the bug. You start off with a manageable quantity and soon the swelling can population takes over your house. I know of collectors who have gotten so carried away that neat rows of beer cans cover the walls and ceilings of their recreation rooms and sometimes their living rooms and bedrooms, too.

The largest collection exceeds 10,000 different cans, which is an attainable number because virtually every brand of beer repeatedly undergoes label design changes. Even the subtlest change, such as changing one word in a phrase set in six-point type creates a new collectible.

Not all cans are equally prized. Scarcity, age and condition help determine whether one is worthless (as are current vintage Miller and Budweiser cans) or worth a thousand dollars or more. Among the most sought after are the 1935 metal containers for Krueger's Finest Beer and Krueger's Cream Ale—the world's first two beer cans. A container that has hit the fancy of many collectors is the Pittsburgh Brewing Company's Olde Frothingslosh with its tongue-in-cheek label featuring an overweight "beauty queen" posing Miss America style in a swimsuit. In Sweden, I've seen X-rated beer cans, complete with erotic nude models. In Chicago a number of years back, I drank a can of my namesake's beer. "Hillman's Superb Brew." It wasn't superb, but I wish that I had kept the can of that now extinct brewery.

Breweriana is an organized hobby. Beer Can Collectors of America, the largest entity of its kind, has 20,000 members and many local chapters. The BCCA facilitates trades among its members through its monthly magazine, bi-monthly Want Ad Bulletin, membership roster and *Guide to United States Beer Cans* book. It also holds an annual "canvention" where attendees can swap cans, hellos and information. For more details about this nonprofit association, write BCCA, 747 Merus Court, Fenton, Missouri 63026. Another organization worth exploring is the American Breweriana Association (P.O. Box 6082, Colorado Springs, Colorado 80934).

Some enthusiasts don't merely collect beer-related items, they construct objects with them. A woman from Long Island made a glistening gown out of 5,000 aluminum beer can tab tops. Australians have held regattas with replicas of Viking longboats and other multicrew crafts made of empty beer cans.

The biggest breweriana buffs of all, of course, are firms like Stroh and Heileman. By means of mergers and takeovers, they have been collecting full-sized breweries!

A WHIRLWIND TOUR

A travel agent once asked me to suggest an itinerary for a tour of celebrated American and European watering holes. That was a tall order because there are so many exciting beer halls, pubs, bar and taverns that I have had the good fortune to visit. After a little arm twisting on his part, I gave him this list. (If I left off one of your favorites, write me and I'll try to include it in the next edition of this book.)

My suggested journey begins appropriately in Hollywood, my birthplace, where we have a brew in Barney's Beanery. We then proceed to Ichabod's in Denver, Brickskeller in Washington, D.C., and to The Manhattan Brewing Company, McSorley's, New Amsterdam Tap Room, North Star Pub, Peculier Pub, P.J. Clarke's, Suerken's and the White Horse Tavern in New York.

Leaving the States, we head to London where there are so many worthwhile pubs I don't know where to begin. Some of our "must stops" include the Black Friar, The Lamb, Old Mitre, The Princess Louise, The Sun and Ye Olde Cheshire Cheese. Legal pub hours, take note, are brief: 11 A.M. to 3 P.M. and 6 P.M. to 11 P.M. from Monday through Saturday, and noon to 2 P.M. and 7 P.M. to 11 P.M. on Sunday. When the publican shouts "last orders, please," have your glass refilled promptly before he rings the cutoff bell.

Hopping to the Continent, we arrive in Belgium, the home of many fine small breweries including the Trappist variety (See Part Six, p.232). Let's not miss the famous Mort Subite ("sudden death") restaurant in Greater Brussels. Its derives its curious name from a postprandial ritual devised years ago in the restaurant by card-playing factory workers. When they heard the factory whistle calling them back to work from lunch, they hurriedly played one sudden death hand—the winner pocketed all the money on the table.

246

Next we travel to Munich. If we have planned well, we will be there during the 16-day fall Oktoberfest, helping millions of other celebrants wash down countless sausages with millions of liters of beer. There will be song and oom-pah-pah bands galore in the temporary beer tents on the fairgrounds and in the permanent beers halls, including the world famous Hofbräuhaus.

On to Czechoslovakia we go to sip some beer in Pilsen, the home of the celebrated Pilsner Urquell. We then drive to Ceske Budejovice (Budweiss in German) where the original Budweisser is still made. (Anheuser-Busch has to be thankful that this Bohemian brew is not imported into this country because it's significantly superior to the American-made Budweiser.) Our journey ends in the charming 500-year-old U Fleku beerhouse in Prague.

My tour is only on paper. Fortunately, it's easy to design your own private beer tour—Michael Jackson's *World Guide to Beer* is an excellent reference source for planning your adventure. You can also sign up for an organized tour. Ask your local travel agency or write for brochures from these beer-tour organizers: Cole Travel Agency (376 North Main St., Fond du Lac, WI 54935) and Tiberti Travel (177 East 87th St., New York, NY 10028). For current information on beer tours, consult magazines such as *All About Beer*.

You may not have to wear seven-league boots if there's a brewery near your home town. Most local breweries give tours. Free samples are usually given at the end of each tour for those who meet the minimum age requirements, which range from 18 to 21 depending on the state.

More than age limits can change as you cross state lines. Some states allow you to use credit cards for your beer purchases, others insist on cash. Even the retail outlet varies by state: it could be a liquor store, neighborhood grocery or a state run facility.

An alert palate can sometimes detect differences in the alcoholic strengths of the same brands because of varying maximum limits set by the states. (See "The Resulting Alcoholic Strength," p.209). The flavor profile can also change slightly from location to location because the big national brands are brewed in regional plants; ingredients and equipment are never exactly the same. Between Miller and Budweiser, I find that the latter is a more consistent product.

HISTORY AND TRENDS

Beer is older than history. No one knows for sure when it was discovered, but some archaeologists place the date around 25,000 B.C. when, perhaps, some cave dweller accidentally let his leftover porridge ferment during his absence on a three-day hunting trip. The oldest-known written reference to brewing that I know of is on Mesopotamian clay tablets dating back to about 6000 B.C.

In Egypt, I've seen ancient tomb paintings depicting the brewing process. While exploring Karnak along the Nile, I met an archaeologist who brought to my attention hieroglyphics on Mut's gate that said "Beer, red with Nubian ocher, is poured in honor of the goddess."

Beer was a basic food in Egypt and many other Middle Eastern cultures because it was nutritious (more so than today) and more hygienic than the available drinking water. People who drank beer generally lived longer.

The brewers in these early civilizations were, more often than not, women. (In contrast, virtually all the professional brewers in this day and age are men.)

When Hammurabi became king of Babylon around 4,000 years ago, he found it necessary to formulate laws governing the sale of beer. If brewers were found to have diluted their products, they were incarcerated in their own vats. (Let this be an object lesson to modern light beer manufacturers.)

Brewing was not confined to the West. Both in India and China beer was made at least four millennia ago, using rice, barley wheat and millet.

The elite and many of the common citizens of Rome were generally disdainful of beer, preferring instead the gift of Bacchus, fermented grape juice. Nonetheless, it is from the Latin language that we get the English and Spanish names for the beer we drink. "Beer" derives from the Latin word *bibere*, to drink, and *cerveza* (Spanish for beer) from Ceres, the Roman goddess of agriculture.

Wine made significant inroads in many other Mediterranean

lands, but beer remained the most popular alcoholic beverage in northern Europe because its cooler climate was more suited for growing barley and wheat than it was for grapes. (Even today, beer reigns supreme in Northern Europe and wine in Southern Europe, though this geographical distinction is beginning to blur.)

The dietary foundation of the masses in medieval Germany and England was bread and beer. These two foods have so much in common in terms of ingredients and initial preparation that beer has long been called "liquid bread."

Beer was deeply rooted in medieval rites. In England, it was traditional for the bride to serve ale to her gift-bearing guests; the word "bridal" stems from this custom. In Nordic lands, "beer-hall testimony" was legally binding.

Monasteries actively brewed and sold beer. Five hundred years ago some enterprising Bavarian monks discovered that they could make a clearer and more dependable brew in the hot summer months if they aged their *Bier* in wooden casks stored in cold Alpine caverns. We now call their invention "lager" which comes from *lagern*, the German verb "to store."

Another major milestone occurred in 1516. The duke of Bavaria decreed, in the now famous Rheinheitsgebot law, that beer could be made only with barley, hops and water. This Bavarian purity code neglected to mention yeast only because that mysterious fungus was not known to be an ingredient at that time. The world would have to wait until the nineteenth century for Louis Pasteur to reveal the true nature of this microscopic plant.

Though hops have been used to flavor and preserve beer for at least 1,000 years, it was only within the last several centuries that their use became widespread. Earlier brewers typically flavored their beers with ingredients such as herbs and spices.

Per capita consumption for both royalty and the common folk was much higher in the old days than currently. Queen Elizabeth I (1533-1603) not only drank copious quantities herself, she gave a massive daily beer allowance to each of her ladies-in-waiting.

In the Americas, beer predates Columbus. The Genoan navigator reported that on one of his landings the natives offered him a brew made from corn. We don't know how many stars he awarded it.

I bet you didn't know that it was partially due to beer that the Pilgrims landed in Massachusetts in 1620 rather than father south in a warmer climate as they had originally planned. The crew and passengers decided to curtail their voyage because, as a firsthand written account of the journey inform us, "our victuals were much spent, especially our beer."

Some of our most illustrious Colonial and founding fathers were brewers. William Penn, George Washington and Samuel Adams were all brewers, and Thomas Jefferson was a dedicated student of the art and science of brewing. In those days, brewing was encouraged as an industry and beer drinking as an exercise in temperance.

The stronger, darker, fuller-bodied English style ales were America's favorite brews. That began to change in the 1840s when German immigrants—including Anheuser, Busch, Pabst, Schaefer and Schlitz—opened breweries producing the lagers of their homeland.

The mass-production lagering technique these gentlemen introduced to America was first perfected in the early nineteenth century by scientifically minded brewmasters from Pilsen, Munich, Vienna and other *Mittel Europa* cities. Because these "new" beers were clearer and lighter, as well as better shippers and storers than existing ales, the lager fad quickly spread throughout most of the world, eventually eclipsing ale as mankind's most popular alcoholic beverage. (In the United States, lagers now account for more than 90% of the beers we consume. Ale still reigns supreme in only a few areas of the world, including the British Isles and parts of Germany and Belgium.)

The number of American breweries reached its apogee in the 1870s; several thousand existed. In the next half century, as individual brewing plants became larger, the count dwindled to roughly 1,500.

On January 16, 1920, the brewing industry ceased to exist, at least in the legal sense. That was the date the infamous Volstead Act took effect and Prohibition was off and running. During the nearly fourteen years of the Great Experiment, Americans drank homemade and bootlegged brew by the barrelful.

Some brewers survived by producing nonalcoholic beverages such as near beer or soda pop. Others moved to Canada where brewing was legal. When the Act was repealed on December 5, 1933, fewer than half of the pre-Prohibition breweries resumed operations in America.

Recent History

The average beer brewed in the few years after Repeal typically contained 50% more malt and 250% more hops than its current counterparts. (In fact, the ordinary beer of that period was as flavorful as the super premiums of today.) Over this same half-century span, the body of the average beer has thinned only slightly and the alcoholic strength has remained relatively stable.

World War II helped seal the doom of many regional breweries and accelerated the trend toward blander and lighter beers. Many of the returning young servicemen, after having been weaned on the insipid and uniform 3.2 generic beer that came in olive drab cans, formed a ready market for the emerging national brands that lacked distinctive regional character. Regrettably, the number who both encountered and brought back with them a developed appreciation of the flavorful Northern European brews was few.

Also contributing to the predominance of the national brands was the growth of the supermarket chain system. Major chains that sold beer found it easier to merchandise a few national brands than a lot of regional or local ones. Another factor was the increasing mobility of the American society. People who moved from Maine to California, for instance, were more likely to place a familiar than an unknown brand into their shopping carts.

In the 1950s, brewing became a near-exact science. Thanks to advances in microbiology and equipment technology, modern brewers were able to eliminate or control, for the first time, virtually all the possible variables that could cause a defective beer. Before the process was so scientifically governed, brewing was a chancy enterprise full of unwanted surprises.

On June 12, 1969, a month before man first landed on the moon, the age of takeovers and mergers began in earnest in the brewing industry. That was the date the cigarette giant Philip Morris inhaled Miller Brewing Co. Since then, Schaefer and Schlitz became part of Stroh, Ranier and Carling part of Heileman, Olympia part of Pabst, Pearl part of Falstaff, and Rheingold part of C. Schmidt & Sons of Philadelphia. This scrambling for dominance has attracted the attention of the Justice Department's Antitrust Division.

Takeovers and mergers have concentrated the American brewing industry. Since the repeal of Prohibition, the number of brewing firms plummeted from about 750 to forty, and the top ten firms now brew 95% of the domestic output. The top two, Anheuser-Busch and Miller, have cornered more than half the market.

The rationale for these consolidations has been economy of scale: behemoth breweries can better compete in terms of production, distribution and advertising. For instance, the cost per 1,000 viewers for showing an advertisement on national television is significantly less than on regional or local television. Acquisitions also allow firms like Stroh to expand and strengthen their existing distribution networks—and to augment their plant capacity at distress sale prices.

As the national brands increased their dominance of the marketplace, polished Madison Avenue advertising skills became essential. After all, what distinguishes one taste-alike national brand from another is largely product image created by sleek television commercials. In recent years, Anheuser-Busch alone spent about $100 million per annum on advertising to induce us to buy its products.

Brewers are also laying out unprecedented sums to sponsor highly visible rock concerts, jazz festivals and sport events. Anheuser-Busch again took the lead by committing $10 million to become the official beer of the 1984 Summer Olympics in Los Angeles.

A few middle-size breweries managed to survive and not be gobbled up mainly because they tailored their products to the local or regional taste and pushed their brands selectively to well-targeted audiences, something the big national brands cannot do profitably.

In recent times, some brewers have attempted to increase profits by tampering with the quality of their brew. The classic case is Schlitz, which decided in the mid-70s to cut ingredient costs and to abbreviate its brewing process. Many of Schlitz's loyal customers were obviously not fooled; sales dropped by more than half in five years. A new management team reinstituted the old ways, but Humpty Dumpty had already fallen.

American-style light beers are a relatively new phenomenon. Though the DuBois Brewing Company marketed its "famous light beer" in 1940, the charge of the light brigade did not begin to gain momentum until Gablinger's hit the marketplace in the 1960s.

It was not until 1975, however, that the sales of light beers began to gallop. The Miller Brewing Company purchased the "Lite" trademark from the sinking Meister Brau brewery. The marketing gurus knew that there was a trend in America toward anything light, irrespective of quality. But, they had a problem. Few heavy beer drinkers were concerned about their weight, and few calorie-conscious individuals would even consider beer in their weight-reduction diets. Someone came up with a dandy strategy: Why not create a TV advertising campaign featuring aging sports heroes promoting the theme that you can drink more of Miller's Lite because it is less filling? The macho-oriented commercials were targeted at young, adult males who loved watching sports in front of the tube. This message hit a responsive chord and the rest is history. Lite beer from Miller and the other light beers now account for about 15% of the beer sold in this country. Even in tradition-bound England and Germany I've noticed that light beer is starting to make commercial headway. Is nothing sacred?

Savvy advertisers are paying close attention to demographics. Their targeted consumer is the upwardly mobile, under-thirty-five, well-educated urban dweller of any sex or race. Older drinkers are comparatively poor targets—they are more set in their ways and are less likely to switch brands let alone try a new one.

As the prevalence of national brands and advertising has grown, so has annual per capita consumption of beer. Over the last two decades, it has risen in America from 60 quarts in 1960 to approximately 100 quarts today (compared to 10 quarts each for wine and spirits). West Germany leads the world with 160 quarts. The other ten nations that currently outdrink us are Australia, Austria, Belgium, Czechoslovakia, Denmark, East Germany, Great Britain, Ireland, Luxembourg and New Zealand.

Beer's share of commercial beverage consumption in the United States has risen dramatically over the last two decades, from roughly 13% in 1962 to 20% today. In the same period, milk's share has declined from approximately 29% to 20% and coffee's from about 33% to 18%.

In the 1970s, imported beer sales started to take off, particularly in New York and a few other large metropolitan areas. The causes behind this zoom in sales are many: the gourmet food and wine boom set the stage for the appreciation of fine beers; college students became imported beer aficionados and continued to be so in their postschool lives; travelers to Europe developed a liking for the flavorful European beers; beer drinking became more socially acceptable in fine restaurants because imported beers have cachet; ethnic restaurants spurred interest in imported brews; and the new generation of women beer drinkers expanded the market for quality beers. Also, let's not overlook the fact that most imported beers are superior to most domestic ones.

Within the last ten years microbreweries have been mushrooming across America producing beers that often match the excellence of the better European imports. Some of the so-called boutique brands like Red Hook Ale in Seattle, Washington are produced in such small quantities that their sales are exclusively or almost totally restricted to draft sales to local bars.

By strict definition, microbreweries have production capacities of less than 10,000 barrels a year. The celebrated Anchor Steam Brewing Company, however, is still commonly considered a microbrewery even though it has a 25,000 barrel capacity. Nevertheless, that figure is minute compared to the 60,000,000 annual barrel production capacity of Anheuser-Busch.

The surge in interest in quality beers has spawned a number of special interest publications. For the devoted beer lover there is the informative *All About Beer*. This magazine and other worthwhile publications are listed in the Bibliography.

Trends

The public's image of beer drinkers and drinking is altering. Fading is the Sam Six-Pack stereotype, the undershirted, pot-bellied slob who sits mesmerized for hours guzzling brew in front of a television set. Today when you think of a beer drinker, you are just as apt to see in your mind's eye a young upscale couple sipping imported quality beer at a swank restaurant.

More Americans are truly tasting beer for the first time in their lives. Rather than swigging, they are savoring the beer in their hand, contemplating its strengths and weaknesses. This discriminating group represents only 5% of the public, but that figure equates to more than 10 million people, a sizable market.

Many knowledgeable wine drinkers are becoming beer connoisseurs as well because they recognize that each beverage at its best has a place in gastronomy. To them, it is not so much a question of "which is better?" as "which would please me the most in this given set of circumstances?"

Women will become an ever more important segment of the market. This will be especially true with super premium and imported beers.

Restaurants and bars will discover that they can no longer merely stock a few imported beers if they want to attract and keep the patronage of the increasingly sophisticated American diner. Having a product or two from a domestic microbrewery will help, too.

Two-thirds of the imported beer we drink is consumed in bars, restaurants and other on-premise consumption sites. The other third is purchased at stores and other off-premise locations for home consumption. (For domestic brews, the exact opposite occurs.) In the future, the percentage of imported beers that Americans take home to their refrigerators will grow.

Brewers will create new-style beers targeted to special audiences. Most of these "concept brews" will enter the marketplace with alot of hype and hoopla, but will eventually fail or stumble, as was the case with the low-alcohol brands aimed primarily at people who are concerned about driving under the influence of alcohol.

Although low-alcohol beer sales have not lived up to expectations, the concern about drunk driving will intensify. So will public concern over litter. Expect to see more states enacting bottle-return laws.

Consumer groups will prompt many state legislatures to require brewers to list information such as ingredients and alcoholic content on their labels.

There is going to be an underground consumer backlash against the bland, sweetish and gassy beers predominant in America. A consumer revolt has already occurrred in England in the form of CAMRA (Campaign for Real Ale), an organization that aroused the public's awareness that natural brews were being replaced with high-tech beers of less character.

Brew pubs like those in England will pop up across the country, state laws permitting. They will be small operations that make beer for consumption on their premises.

Beer snobs will multiply, much as wine snobs did when wine started to become fashionable a decade ago. They will praise and condemn those beers that are deemed proper to like and dislike, and will bore us to death with the memorized details.

The reins of the once conservatively run brewing industry are being firmly taken over by highly skilled and talented finance and marketing types. Incoming brewmasters will be chemistry whizzes.

By 1990, Anheuser-Busch and Miller will have together carved out two-thirds of the domestic market. Mergers and takeovers will continue because there is room for only two or three national breweries with sufficient economic clout to compete with these two giants. Consequently, among the remaining eight major breweries on the current top ten list, it is going to be the survival of the fittest. Expect some dirty infighting.

Imported beers will continue to expand their share of the American market. By 1990 that portion is expected to be 6 to 8% (several billion dollars in annual sales).

Nearly two-thirds of import sales in the States are currently concentrated in five major markets; New York accounts for almost one-third of the total. This will change as other markets join the imported beer boom.

Of the 400+ brands imported into this country, the top twenty command 95% of the imported beer market. In the shakeout period that will surely occur within the next five years, the imported beer market will become even more concentrated with less than ten beers garnering the same 95%. Hundreds of other brands, though, will still be able to secure small market niches by appealing to special tastes and interests.

More of the imported brands will be custom-brewed to suit the perceived American taste. Regrettably, these beers will be less flavorful than those consumed in their countries of origin.

Other "imported" brands will be brewed Stateside either in plants operated for the foreign brewer, or—as Löwenbräu did with Miller—under a licensing arrangement with an American firm. Their logic: why ship water across the ocean? (Beer is 90% water.) Unfortunately, a quality beer suffers when its brewing formula and process is transplanted from its homeland.

TOASTS

When drinking an imported beer, it's a nice touch to be able to make a toast in the brewer's tongue. Here are some popular toasts (along with their phonetic pronunciations) that I learned in several dozen countries that export beer to America:

AUSTRALIA: *Cheers!*
AUSTRIA: *Prost!* (prohst)
BELGIUM (Flemish): *Gezondheid!* (huh-zohnd'-hayt)
BRAZIL: *Saúde!* (sah-ood'-deh)
CANADA (English): *Cheers!*
CANADA (French): *A votre santé* (ah voh'truh sahn-tay')
CHINA (Cantonese): *Yam sing!* (yahm-sing)
COLOMBIA: *Salud!* (sah-lood')
CZECHOSLOVAKIA: *Na zravi!* (nahz-drah-vee)
DENMARK: *Skaål!* (skohl)
ENGLAND: *Cheers!*
FINLAND: *Kippis!* (kip-piss)
FRANCE: *A votre santé!* (ah voh'truh sahn-tay')
GERMANY: *Prost!* (prohst)
GREECE: *Stin igia sou!* (steen ee-yah' soo)
HONG KONG: *Ya sing!* (yahm-sing)
INDIA: *Aap ki shubh kai liyai!* (ahp kay shoob kay lee-aye)
IRELAND (Gaelic): *Slainte!* (slahn-chah)
ISRAEL: *Le'chayim!* (leh-hye'-yim)
ITALY: *Cin cin!* (chin chin)
JAMAICA: *Cheers!*

JAPAN: *Kan pai!* (kahn pye)
KOREA: *Deupstita!* (doop'see-dah')
LUXEMBOURG: *Prost!* (prohst)
MEXICO: *Salud!* (sah-lood')
NETHERLANDS: *Proost!* (prohst)
NEW ZEALAND: *Cheers!*
NORWAY: *Skaål!* (skohl)
PAKISTAN: *Jama Sihap!* (jah-may say-ahp)
PERU: *Salud!* (sah-lood')
PHILIPPINES: *Mabuhay!* (mah-boo-hye')
POLAND: *Na Zdrowie!* (nahz'droh'-vee'ah)
PORTUGAL: *Saúde!* (sah-ood'-deh)
SCOTLAND (Gaelic): *Slainte!* (slahn-chah)
SINGAPORE: *Yam sing!* (yahm-sing)
SOUTH AFRICA (Afrikaans): *Gezondheid!* (huh-zohnd'-hayt)
SOUTH AFRICA (English): *Cheers!*
SPAIN: *Salud!* (sah-lood')
SWEDEN: *Skaål!* (skohl)
TAHITI: *Manuta!* (mah-nuh-tah)
TAIWAN: *Gun Bi!* (gun-bee)
THAILAND: *Chai yo!* (chye-yoh)
YUGOSLAVIA: *Ziveli!* (zhehv'-eh-lee)

I also would like to share with you some of the wit and wisdom that I've heard used as toasts at congenial gatherings here and in England:

> I wish you a Malty Christmas
> And a Hoppy New Year,
> A pocket full of money
> And a cellar full of beer!

> Here's to abstinence—as long as it's
> practiced in moderation.

> May the friends of our youth be the
> companions of our old age.

> A stein in the hand is worth two on the bar.

> Love to one, friendship to many, and good
> will to all.

May you always have a full belly, a heavy
purse, and a light heart.

Eat, drink and be merry, for tomorrow we diet.

Two ins and one out: in health, in wealth
and out of debt.

May we look back on the past with as much
pleasure as we look forward to the future.

May you live as long as you want, may you
never want as long as you live.

To my spouse and lover—may they never meet.

BIBLIOGRAPHY

SUGGESTED READING

Books

All About Beer by John Porter (1975, Doubleday and Company, New York).

American Breweries by Donald Bull et al. (1984, Bullworks, Trumbull, Connecticut).

The Art of Making Beer by Stanley F. Anderson with Raymond Hull (1971, Hawthorn Books, New York).

Beer Advertising Openers—A Pictorial Guide by Donald A. Bull (Available from the author at P.O. Box 106, Trumbull, Connecticut 06611).

Beer and Brewing, a home-brewing primer by Dave Laing and John Hendra (1977, Macdonald Educational Ltd., London).

Beer and Wine Making Illustrated Dictionary by Leo Zanelli (1979, Kaye and Ward, London).

The Beer Book by Bob Abel (1981, Quick Fox, New York).

The Beer Book by Will Anderson (1973, Pyne Press, Princeton, New Jersey).

The Beer Can by The Beer Can Collectors of America, edited by Larry Wright (1976, Cornerstone Library, New York).

Beer Can Collecting by Lew Cady (Available from the author at P.O. Box 2, Central City, Colorado 80427).

Beer Can Collector's Bible by Jack Martello (1976, Ballantine Books, New York).

Beer Cans Unlimited, 1980 Edition by Art and Pete Ressel, edited by Robert L. Dabbs (1980, Maverick Publishing Co., Buckner, Missouri).

Beer Drinking in Madison by Warsaw Strohs et al. (1983, Warsaw Strohs, Madison, Wisconsin).

Beer Games II by Andy Griscom et al. (1986, Mustang Publishing, New Haven, Connecticut).

The Beer Industry, a volume of trade statistics edited by Jerry Steinman (1982, Beer Marketer's Insights, West Nyack, New York).

Beer Naturally, a treatise on traditional British ale by Michael Hardman and Theo Bergstrom (1978, Bergstrom-Boyle Books Limited, London).

Beer Trivia by Donald Bull (1985, Beaufort Books, New York).

Beer, USA by William Anderson (Available from the author at 291 Garfield Place, Brooklyn, New York)

Better Beer & How to Brew It by M.R. Reese (1981, Garden Way Publishing, Charlotte, Vermont).

The Big Book of Brewing by Dave Line (1982, Amateur Wine-maker Publications, Ltd., Andover, Hampshire, England).

Brewers Almanac, a loose-leaf book of trade statistics and regulations (1982, United States Brewers Association, Inc., Washington, D.C.).

Brewery Handbook, a textbook for the professional brewer (De Laval Separator Co., St. Louis, Missouri).

Brewing in Canada by Brewers Association of Canada (1965, Ottawa, Ontario).

Brewing Lager Beer by Gregory Noonan (1986, Brewers Publications, Boulder, Colorado).

Brewing Mead by Robert Gayre and Charlie Papazian (1986, Brewers Publications, Boulder, Colorado).

Brewing Science, Volumes I and II, texts for the professional brewer edited by J.R.A. Pollock (1979 and 1981, Academic Press, New York).

Chemical Additives in Booze by Michael Lipske (1982, Center for Science in the Public Interest, Washington, D.C.).

The Class Book of U.S. Beer Cans (Class Publishing Company, Colmar, Pennsylvania).

The Complete Book of Beer Drinking Games by Andy Griscom et al., (RJ Publications, New Haven, Connecticut).

The Complete Joy of Home Brewing by Charlie Papazian (1984, Avon, New York).

Connoisseur's Guide to Beer by James D. Robertson (1985, Caroline House Publishing, Aurora, Illinois).

Cooking with Beer by Carol Fahy (1972, Dover Publications, New York).

Cooking with Beer by Annette Ashlock Stover and The Culinary Arts Institute Staff (1980, Delair Publishing Company, New York).

Falstaff's Complete Beer Book by Frederic Birmingham (1970, Award Books, New York).

Foreign Beer Cans by Darrold Bussell (Available from the author at 2046 N. Raisinville Road, Monroe, Michigan 48161).

The Great American Beer Book, a primer by James D. Robertson (1978, Caroline House Publishers, Inc., Aurora, Illinois).

The Great Beer Trek by Stephen Morris (1984, Stephen Greene Press, Brattleboro, Vermont).

The Great Canadian Beer Book, edited by Gerald Donaldson and Gerald Lampert (1975, McClelland and Stewart Limited, Toronto).

Guide to United States Beer Cans prepared by The Beer Can Collectors of America (1975, Greatlakes Living Press, Matteson, Illinois).

A History of Brewing by H.S. Corran (1975, David & Charles, Inc., North Pomfret, Vermont).

Home Beermaking by Brian Leverett (1980, Prism Press, Dorset, England).

Home Beermaking, The Complete Beginner's Guide by William Moore (1980, Ferment Press, P.O. Box 461, Oakland, California).

Home Brewed Beer & Cider by Ben Turner (1981, EP Publishing, Yorkshire, England).

Home Brewing for Americans by David Miller (Amateur Winemaker Publications Ltd., Andover, Hampshire, England).

Home Brewing Without Failures by H.E. Bravery (1965, Gramercy Publishing Company, New York).

How-to-Build a Small Brewery, a home-brewing primer by Bill Owens (1982, Working Press, Livermore, California).

The International Book of Beer Can Collecting by Richard Dolphin (1979, Book Sales, Inc., Secaucus, New Jersey).

An Introduction to Brewing Science and Technology, Parts I, II and III, texts for the professional brewer edited by C. Rainbow and G.E.S. Float (1981, The Institute of Brewing, London).

Malting and Brewing Science, Volumes I and II, texts for the professional brewer by D.E. Briggs et al. (1981, Chapman and Hall, New York).

Microbrewers Resource Directory, edited by Stuart Harris (1983, Distributed by American Homebrewers Association, P.O. Box 287, Boulder, Colorado 80306).

Miniature Beer Bottles and Go-Withs by Robert E. Kay (1980, K & K Publishers, Batavia, Illinois).

Modern Brewery Age Blue Book, an annual source book that has become one of the bibles in the beer trade (Business Journals Inc., Norwalk, Connecticut).

The New Brew It Yourself by Leigh P. Beadle (1981, Farrar, Straus and Giroux, New York).

The New Brewers Handbook, a booklet for the home brewer by Patrick Baker (1979, Crosby & Baker Books, Westport, Massachusetts).

The New Revised and More Joy of Brewing, a home-brewing primer by Charlie Papazian (Available from the author at P.O. Box 1825, Boulder, Colorado 80306).

One Hundred Years of Brewing, a history (1903, H.S. Rich & Company, Chicago).

The Penguin Guide to Real Draught Beer by Michael Dunn (1979, Penguin Books, New York).

The Pocket Guide to Beer by Michael Jackson (1986, Simon & Schuster, New York).

Practical Beermaking for Beginners by Jim Weathers (Home Fermenter Publications, San Leandro, California).

The Practical Brewer, 2nd Edition, a textbook for professional brewers edited by Harold M. Broderick (1977, Master Brewers Association of the Americas, Madison, Wisconsin).

A Price Guide to Beer Advertising Openers and Corkscrews by Donald A. Bull (Available from the author at P.O. Box 106, Trumbull, Connecticut 06611).

Quality Brewing, a home-brewing primer by Byron Burch (1980, Joby Books, San Rafael, California).

The Register of United States Breweries 1876—1976 by Manfred Friedrich & Donald Bull (1976, Available from Donald Bull, P.O. Box 106, Trumbull, Connecticut 06611).

Special Information Book, a summary of state laws and regulations (1983, United States Brewers Association, Washington, D.C.).

Steiner's Guide to American Hops (1973, S.S. Steiner, Inc., New York).

A Taste of the West from Coors, a cookbook edited by Anita Krajeski (1981, Meredith Publishing Services, Des Moines, Iowa).

Tavern Treasures by Charles E. Tresise (1983, Blandford Press, Dorset, England).

A Treatise on Lager Beer, a home-brewing primer by Fred Eckhardt (1981, Hobby Winemaker, Portland, Oregon).

The Taster's Guide to Beer by Michael A. Weiner (1977, Collier Books, New York).

20 Years of American Beers, The '30s and '40s by Reino Ojala (Available from the author at P.O. Box 1121, Burnsville, Minnesota 55337).

The U.S. Beer Coaster Guide, Volume I by Thomas Byrne (Available from the author at P.O. Box 173, East Hanover, New Jersey 07936).

The World Guide to Beer by Michael Jackson (1977, Prentice-Hall, Inc., Englewood Cliffs, New Jersey).

Periodicals

Alephenalia, a tabloid published periodically (Merchant du Vin, Seattle, Washington).

All About Beer, a monthly magazine for beer drinkers (McMullen Publishing, Inc., Anaheim, California).

Amateur Brewer, a quarterly magazine (Hayward, California 94541-0713).

American Breweriana Journal, a bimonthly magazine published by American Breweriana Association (A.B.A., P.O. Box 6082, Colorado Springs, Colorado 80934)

The American Can Collector, a monthly tabloid for the collector (Available from Jim Hunter, P.O. Box 608, Mt. Home, Arkansas 72653).

Beer Can Collectors News Report, a bimonthly magazine published by Beer Can Collectors of America (747 Merus Court, Fenton, Missouri).

Beer Marketer's Insights, a semimonthly newsletter for the beer trade (Jerry Steinman, 55 Virginia Avenue, W. Nyack, New York).

Beer Statistics News, a semimonthly newsletter for the beer trade (Beer Marketer's Insights, Inc., W. Nyack, New York).

Beverage Communicator, a quarterly magazine for the home wine and beer supply retailer (Beverage Communicator, P.O. Box 43, Hartsdale, New York).

Brewers Bulletin, a semiweekly trade publication (P.O. Box 906, Woodstock, Illinois 60098).

Brewer's Digest, a monthly trade publication for the professional brewer (Siebel Publishing, Chicago, Illinois).

Brewery Collectibles Magazine, a bimonthly publication (Class Publishing Co., P.O. Box 43, Colmar, Pennsylvania 18915).

The Canadian Brewerianist, a monthly publication (The Canadian Brewerianist, 2978 Lakeview Trail, Bright's Grove, Ontario NON 1CO Canada).

Home Fermenter's Digest, a quarterly magazine for home beer and wine makers (Hayward, California 94541-0713).

Journal of the American Society of Brewing Chemists, quarterly technical journal for professional brewers (The American Society of Brewing Chemists, St. Paul, Minnesota).

Listen to Your Beer, bimonthly newsletter for the beer drinker (ABIS, P.O. Box 546, Portland, Oregon 97207).

The MBAA Technical Quarterly, technical journal for the members (Master Brewers Association of the Americas, Madison, Wisconsin).

Modern Brewery Age, monthly journal for brewers and wholesalers (Business Journals Inc., Norwalk, Connecticut).

The New Brewer, a bimonthly magazine published by the Institute for Fermentation and Brewing Studies (Boulder, Colorado 80306-0287).

Newsletter of The American Society of Brewing Chemists, quarterly newsletter for the professional brewer (American Society of Brewing Chemists, St. Paul, Minnesota).

What's Brewing, monthly tabloid for the beer drinker by The Campaign for Real Ale (What's Brewing, 34 Alma Street, St. Albans, Hertfordshire, England, AL 1 3 BW).

Zymurgy, quarterly journal for home brewers (American Home Brewers Association, Boulder, Colorado).

ABOUT THE AUTHOR

World traveler Howard Hillman has searched the globe for interesting beers. He has evaluated over 5,000 different brews during his many research trips that have taken him to over one hundred countries, from Afghanistan to Zimbabwe. There is hardly a brew that has not touched his lips.

Hillman lectures on brew, conducts gourmet beer tastings and is often interviewed by the television, radio and print media for his expertise.

He has written more than twenty-five books including *The Art of Dining Out, The Diner's Guide to Wines, Great Peasant Dishes of the World, The Cook's Book, Kitchen Science, Howard Hillman's Kitchen Secrets, The Book of World Cuisines* and a nationwide series of dining out guidebooks to major American cities.

Howard Hillman's works have been critically praised, selected by book clubs and designated "Outstanding Reference Boooks" by both the American Library Association and the Library Journal. His works have been translated into Braille and foreign languages.

His bylined articles and columns have been published in *Newsweek, The New York Times, Washington Post, Chicago Tribune, The Wall Street Journal, Cook's Magazine, Food & Wine* and other major publications.

Howard Hillman, a Harvard M.B.A., has an extensive business background that includes the presidency of the National Academy of Sports and vice presidency of the American Film Theatre.

INDEX

Brands of beer appear, in alphabetical order, in the section on rating beers, pp. 71-193, but are not included in this index.